From Survivor to Thriver

The Story of a Modern Day Tin Man

by Brian Campkin

Motivational PRESS®
LEADERS IN GLOBAL PUBLISHING

Published by Motivational Press, Inc.
7777 N Wickham Rd, # 12-247
Melbourne, FL 32940
www.MotivationalPress.com

Manufactured in the United States of America.

ISBN: 978-1-62865-145-4

Contents

DEDICATION

To my wife and best friend Lori who shared this journey with me every step of the way. I could not have made it without your unparalleled support and love.

To my three daughters, Megan, Julie and Kelly who were my motivation and inspiration on every step of my journey.

To my good friend June Rogers whose constant support and coaching enabled me to have the confidence and motivation to write this book. She saw and believed in me what I could not see in myself.

And lastly, to my Dad, Lawrence Ford Campkin and my good friend, Mike Fox, who were taken by this dreadful disease in the prime of their lives. This book is for them and everyone who has succumbed to this disease long before their journey on this earth was complete.

FOREWARD

At the Heart and Stroke Foundation, we often use figures to demonstrate the impact we're having on the heart health of Canadians. We've invested over $1.4 billion in live-saving and life-giving heart disease and stroke research since our inception.

We're also proud of (and grateful for) the Foundation's 140,000 volunteers who carry our message and spread hope. We also frequently stress that well over 1.3 million Canadians are currently living with the effects of heart disease and stroke.

While such figures raise eyebrows and demonstrate the need for our programs and our commitment to reducing heart disease and stroke, there are few things more powerful than an individual's story.

Brian Campkin has chosen to share his story of survival and his journey of recovery – a selfless act that will surely benefit anyone who reads these pages. He is candid about his fears, his doubts, his physical and mental setbacks and ultimately, his triumphs. You see heart disease through his eyes.

His story touches on so many important themes we try to emphasize at the Foundation. One such theme is how heart disease and stroke affects the entire family.

Brian's story includes first-hand accounts from his wife and his children who are equally candid as they express their thoughts and feelings about their father's illness. It's quite powerful to read what a daughter thinks of her father having to undergo heart surgery. His wife's apprehensions of having to play the role of caregiver and the need to take care of her own health under stressful conditions will also connect with anyone who has cared for a loved one.

His story also dispels a myth that heart disease and stroke is an "old man's disease." Nothing could be further from the truth, as Brian, a seemingly healthy man in his mid-forties who never smoked, ate well and played competitive tennis, clearly shows.

When reading this book, the power of a having a positive attitude also resonates. It's clear that Brian made a decision to focus on what he could achieve, not what he has lost. His positive attitude, even while awaiting news in doctors' offices or even in a hospital bed, echoes throughout this book and the importance of his mindset throughout his recovery cannot be measured.

Along his journey, Brian found strength in sharing his story and has become a popular volunteer and survivor speaker. I can't thank him enough for all he has done for the Foundation.

With an infectious energy and spirit, every audience he connects with is touched, moved and motivated to either approach heart disease and stroke recovery with a newfound energy, or inspired to live a healthier lifestyle in order to prevent these diseases.

Personally, what impresses me most with Brian and his recovery is his decisiveness. He chose to act. He set out clear measurable goals and then set out a plan to achieve them. And it's been an absolute pleasure witnessing each milestone.

They started out small, like walking one crack in the sidewalk further and have since become life-changing joys, like being a grandparent. He is truly relishing each day of what he calls "an awesome second chance at life."

Like Brian, we too have ambitious goals at the Foundation. By the year 2020, we hope to significantly improve the health of Canadians by decreasing their risk factors for heart disease and stroke by 10 per cent. We also expect to reduce Canadians' rate of death from heart disease and stroke by 25 per cent by that same year.

Working with people like Brian and seeing him enjoying a healthy, active and rich life reinforces our belief that we *can* create healthy lives free of heart disease and stroke. Together, we *will* make it happen.

David Sculthorpe, CEO,
Heart and Stroke Foundation of Canada

INTRODUCTION

"In life it's 10% what happens to you
and 90% how you react to it."

~ Irving Berlin
American composer, 1888 – 1989.

When we are young, we think that life will go on forever and we have so much ahead of us; our dreams, our passions and our family. Suddenly, without a moment's notice all of this can change..

It seems like only yesterday when my Dad left for a short vacation to Florida in the winter of 1991. He normally went for a couple of months and I would always hug him and tell him how much I loved him. But this time, he was going for a couple of weeks; so when he left, I just punched him in the arm and said, "See you soon Dad, see you soon!" Then, I received that fateful call on March 7th - the day before he was to come home from his vacation. He had suffered a massive heart attack and died.

I never realized that would be my last message to him - I miss my Dad, I miss him so much. In an instant, I had lost my mentor, my best friend and my Dad forever.

Ensuring that I am there for my family for years to come is a big part of the reason why I have always taken care of myself physically; I wanted to ensure that my three daughters were not robbed of valuable "Dad" time as I was.

But my Dad was from a different era than the one we live in today. He wasn't as health conscious as we are today. He was a smoker and didn't exercise. He wasn't like me. I was different: I ate healthy, never smoked and played tennis. I was your classic weekend-warrior when it came to exercise. I played hockey, baseball, tennis and biked occasionally.

I was on the tennis court when it happened. Suddenly, I was out of breath for the first time ever. It really put the fear of dying into me. I was scared and didn't know what was wrong with me. Luckily, I managed to walk off the tennis court and make it to my doctor. He sent me in for a series of tests. After five weeks, an angiogram determined that three of my four main arteries were 100% blocked. I was barely firing on one cylinder and needed an emergency triple by-pass surgery. The universe flipped a coin - I got lucky but my Dad didn't.

The Heart and Stroke Foundation of Canada states that 50% percent of people, who are diagnosed with heart disease, that their first symptom is death!

Almost 29% of all deaths in Canada are due to cardiovascular disease, which comes to a staggering 69,000 deaths a year. My story is unique because of my belief in life after the knife. I planned to fully take advantage of my second chance at life. My story will share with you the trials, tribulations and the milestones I was able to achieve.

I will be telling you my story in two different tones. One as the voice of prevention for those who have never been struck with heart disease and what you can do to keep yourself on the prevention pathway and two, as the voice of hope for those that have been diagnosed with heart disease.

I know this because I overcame all of the self-doubt and pity one would like to have everyone to be a part of. I decided early on in my diagnosis that I wasn't going to be the driver of the bitter bus on its way to pity city. Irving Berlin's quote really spoke to me. I decided that from that moment forward, when - not if, but when - I was back on recovery road, I w̖ take full advantage of my opportunity because at the end of the day, I h one huge life milestone to get to. I wanted to walk each one of my thre̖ daughters down the aisle on their future wedding days.

So settle in, turn the page and get ready to go on a journey of inspiration, perspiration and hope as I take you on an emotional ride from my symptoms and diagnosis to the main event and onto recovery road and beyond.

A young Lawrence Ford Campkin when he was dating my Mom

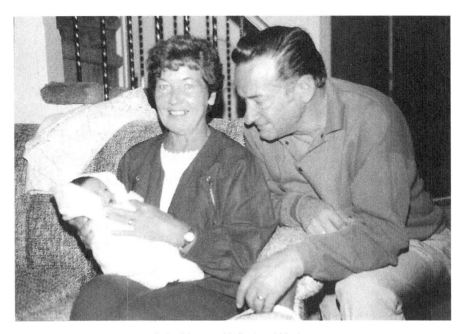

Baby Megan with Dad and Marion

Christmas day 1960 Brian 22 days old

Dad's place in Florida

Lori and I 1977 at a formal dinner we put on

Lori and I in 1978 two years after we met

Me with my 3 siblings,
Debbie, Brad and Cheryl
around 1965

My Dad always loved our family time here he sits on Santa's knee at his last Christmas

Another shot of Dad that last Christmas

My Dad at one of our family events

My favourite photo of my Dad as it was
professionally taken

The Family 1966

With my brother Brad and my sisters Cheryl and Debbie

With my Dad 5 months before his death

With my Dad and Mom on my 14th birthday
with my favourite gift my first authentic Leafs jersey

Chapter 1 – The Symptoms

"Our health always seems much more valuable after we lose it."

- Unknown Author

The new year started off great as we ushered in the new year with family and friends at a dinner and dance gala at a local golf and country club in 2007. Surrounding ourselves with those, who were closest to us, was one of my wife's and my favourite past times; tonight was no different. We spent the evening chatting, dancing and laughing. And then, at the stroke of midnight, as we cheered in the New Year, I felt this sudden breeze behind me as my suit pants tore open from celebrating too much. I thought to myself that it wasn't a very good start to the New Year, but little did I know that this was going to be the smallest of issues that first month of the year.

Our health issues started when the family was stricken with the stomach flu - four out of the five of us were down and out. Shortly after that, I had a chest cold, followed by pink eye and then, an ear infection. Holy smokes! I was starting to wish my life away and began looking forward to February, which wasn't my normal manner of being. But with all of these illnesses, I just wanted to move ahead with my life in a healthier way. Finally, with the ear infection, I gave in and went to the local clinic for some antibiotics. Like most men of my generation, I wasn't a fan of visiting the doctor's office, but I begrudgingly felt that I needed some professional help so to speak. After a long wait and a short consultation, I was provided a prescription and sent on my way.

With all of these illnesses in January, I still continued to play in my weekly tennis league and luckily, I was steadily moving up my tennis ladder to the top of my division, a perch I had never succeeded in claiming. By the end of the month, I actually made it to court number 1 and had the chance to be at the top of my ladder for the first time. I was pretty nervous when I arrived that night because I had never played against the elite guys in our league and tonight would be my big test.

I felt good coming into the match; I had started my antibiotics for my ear infection and all of my other health issues were behind me. I felt for the first time that month that I could play my style of tennis, which was hustle, hustle and hustle some more! There was literally no tennis ball that I felt I could not get my racquet on. OK, so I'm a little bit competitive, but I always had high expectations for myself. As I began warming up with my opponents I immediately realized that something wasn't quite right. I was having difficulty breathing; it was something that I had never experienced before, at least not without chasing down a potential point after a super long rally. I did a quick self-diagnosis and immediately decided that it was just my body reacting to the new antibiotic I was on (I would later call this missing the warning sign #1).

I continued to play my match that night, but truly had some difficulty breathing. Somehow, I was able to maintain my status on court 1, but didn't achieve my goal of being in the top spot. I wasn't sure how I was able to do this as we switched ends after every odd game - I literally went down on one knee to try to catch my breath. Towards the end of match, on one of these breaks, I remember looking up at the roof of the tennis dome and saying to myself, "I wonder what a heart attack feels like!" (This was warning sign #2).

After the match, I spoke about my experience with my brother-in-law, Mike, who also plays in the same league, my sister Debbie and wife Lori, who walk the track around the court as we play. They all had an opinion and none were the same. Their "professional" opinions were:

→ You have pneumonia.

→ It's your ear drugs.

→ You're still recovering.

My immediate thought here was be careful who you get your professional advice from. Obviously, they weren't a nurse or doctor so I shrugged off their commentary. In fact, I knew that it wasn't pneumonia; I've had it before and it didn't feel like this. I did feel that it could be a combination of the other two diagnoses, so I left it at that. However, later that night in bed, I didn't feel right at all. My breathing was weird. I was having bouts of anxiety, sweat, and my arms were tired from tennis.

I woke Lori to tell her how I was feeling and suggested that maybe calling 911 was a good idea. She thought that I was over-reacting and said that she would drive me to the hospital if I felt it was necessary to go to the emergency ward. I thought it through thoroughly for about one second and said, "Nah it's probably nothing." (This was missing warning sign #3). I declined her invitation and spent the balance of the night in a restless sleep.

When I awoke the following morning, I was somewhat tired but feeling fine. It was as if last night was a dream and it had never happened. However, it remained a topic of conversation for us - for my wife that is. I had dismissed it already, but she became quite adamant in wanting me to follow up with a doctor. I ignored her requests in the beginning, which didn't make her very happy. That day, after my "episode", I went to work and parked my car. After a three to four minute walk to the office doors, I realized that I was a bit winded again. I just dismissed it to the cold January day that we were having and went on with my day (I missed another warning sign!).

The balance of my week was fine and went on without incident and before I knew it, we were back at our Tuesday night tennis league. It was finally February and I felt as though I had a new lease on life as all of the January blah's and illnesses were behind me. I was excited to be at my match - I had another chance to come out on top of court 1 and move up to the A-B division for the first time. I was really hoping that my breathing and my lungs wouldn't let me down again. I was half disappointed. I did play well enough to move up to a new division, but darn, if only my breathing didn't keep acting up again.

When I went home that night to tell Lori how excited I was to be moving up in the league, she quickly dismissed it and focused on my inability to breathe properly. I told her that I was actually frustrated with my match and didn't want to play anymore if I was going to continue having these annoying breathing problems. This was her chance when she said, "Brian if I at least make the doctor's appointment for you will you at least go?" I finally gave her the response that she was looking for and said, "Yes!" At last, I listened to my body, my wife and the final warning sign.

What I came to learn after this experience with my symptoms was that I didn't know what I didn't know. I truly felt that heart disease was an old person's illness and had no idea that shortness of breath or winded, as I called it, was a symptom for heart disease. As I set on my journey toward my diagnosis, I truly felt that the beginning of 2007 just wasn't my best start and that I would overcome this quite easily. I felt that being in my mid-forties and in the best health of my life, or so I thought, that a quick prescription of some R & R, or rest and relaxation would be all that I needed. Little did I know how wrong I was? However, I made good on my promise to Lori and set off on my visit with our family doctor.

Another fabulous family event taking a limo to the play Wicked in downtown Toronto.

Dads Birthday 1989, we spent most of our relationship across a cribbage board.

Family Christmas photo 1987 with Dad

Lori and I on NewYear's Eve.

Lori and I with baby Megan in 1987. Talk about proud parents!

With my eldest sister Debbie.

Sibling dinner out with my sisters Debbie and Cheryl along with my brother Brad.

With my brother Brad and newphew Jeff.

Our family photo from Debbie's Wedding in 1977.

My first Christmas post-surgery December 2007

Weekend Waffles

Ingredients

1 cup (250 mL) all purpose flour

1 cup (250 mL) whole wheat flour

2 Tbsp (30 mL) granulated sugar

2 tsp (10 mL) baking powder

½ tsp (2 mL) baking soda

½ tsp (2 mL) ground nutmeg

½ tsp (2 mL) ground cinnamon

2 eggs

1 cup (250 mL) skim milk

1 cup (250 mL) buttermilk*

3 Tbsp (45 mL) canola oil

Directions

Preheat waffle iron. In a large bowl, sift together flour, sugar, baking powder, baking soda, nutmeg and cinnamon. In a small bowl, whisk together eggs, milk, buttermilk and canola oil. Pour wet mixture over flour mixture and stir together. Do not over mix. For each waffle, lightly spray canola oil cooking spray on the waffle iron. Pour about ½ cup – ¾ cup of batter. Bake until golden brown. Makes 14 – 4 ½ x 4 ½ inch (11 x 11 cm) squares.

*In place of buttermilk, use an equivalent amount of sour milk, made by adding 1 Tbsp (15 mL) of lemon juice or vinegar per 1 cup (250 mL) of milk.

Nutrition Analysis – per serving (2 squares)
Calories: 240
Total Fat: 8g
Saturated Fat: 1g
Cholesterol: 60mg
Sodium: 280mg
Carbohydrates: 32g
Fibre: 2g
Protein: 8g

Recipes from the Quick and Healthy Cookbook developed by The Heart and Stroke Foundation and Manitoba Canola Growers Association

Chapter 2 – The Diagnosis

"Time and health are two precious assets that we don't recognize and appreciate until they have been depleted."

- By Denis Waitley
American writer, Born 1933.

When I met with my family doctor that second week of February and told him what was going on, he did the standard things you would expect in an examination room. He listened to my heart, chest and lungs; he actually stated that I sounded normal. I joked that my wife might challenge him on that diagnosis. He chortled, but little did I know that as we continued on our diagnosis destination how much of a joke this would not become. I told my doctor that perhaps with my old age, I was in need of a puffer or something like that. He just smiled and continued with his examination. I then decided to let him do his job and stopped trying to self-diagnosis.

Upon completion, he said that it could be any number of things and to be safe, he wanted to narrow the list down by sending me in for a chest X-ray, blood work, an electro cardiogram (EKG) and an ultra-sound of my heart. I thought to myself, "Geez, this is quite extensive isn't it?" I just shrugged and figured that he was being overly cautious and that it was the best thing he could be doing for me.

When I left the doctor's office, I went to the lower level of the building where the lab was to see if I could get started on some of my tests. I was in luck and was able to get my blood work and my EKG done right then and there, but I had to book the X-ray and ultrasound for a later date. A funny thing happened after my EKG. The technician asked me if I was here because I had a heart attack. I thought that it was an odd question, but quickly let them know that I was not here for anything like that. It was just some routine tests my doctor ordered because I was experiencing some shortness of breath and was most likely a little over stressed. This was the first of many "clues" that would be delivered to me on what my final outcome and diagnosis was going to be. But for now, I was happy being on the path of denial and was just ignoring these little innuendos that came my way.

At this time, I had decided to not play any tennis as I figured out what was wrong with me and move on with my life. To say the least, during this two week period of testing, I was very, very confused about what was going on with my body and my health. On Valentines' Day, I went for my X-ray without any incident or great revelations. I few days later, I went for an ultrasound of my heart and again, it was all routine. I was starting to think that this was leaning towards a quick diagnosis by my doctor and putting me on stress leave. In fact, I was already starting to figure out what I was going to say to my manager at work.

Finally, two weeks after my initial visit, I was back for my results. His first comment was that all of my results seemed fine, except for my EKG, which showed a "blip" in the read out. This was his technical terminology - a blip, what the heck could that mean? I was waiting for him to say that I needed to take a vacation, but he didn't. Man, I was becoming more and more impatient with this whole process and very frustrated to say the least.

Then, I recalled what the EKG technician had said to me after my test. Was I here because I had a heart attack? This news from my doctor was making me very nervous coupled with the fact that he now wanted to send me for a routine stress test to validate what the EKG was showing. I felt like bringing that conversation with the technician up to him, but instead I told him that I was just stressed out due to my new role at work. I also informed him that I had taken myself out of tennis for the past two weeks. He dismissed my first comment with a wave of his hand and a "We'll see." He did say that he felt that there was no reason as to why I couldn't get back to tennis as we did the tests. This made me feel a bit better. If it were something serious, he would never give me the green light to get back on the courts. I went back down to the lab and booked my stress test for March 2, which I thought was crazy because I had been chasing this diagnosis for a month now. The doctor wasn't kidding when he said that I would need to go through a number of tests to see what was wrong with me, if anything at all. I bounced out of the doctor's office knowing that I was able to get back to tennis. I felt really good about myself for the first time in a long time.

The next day, Feb., 27th, I found myself back on the tennis courts and it felt good until I started running around again. I purposely asked to stay in the lower division rather than move up. In hindsight, it was a good thing since I had little to no mobility out on the courts four weeks ago. I was really frustrated and really concerned because I knew in my mind that something just wasn't right. I somehow played well enough to maintain my court #1 status. I don't know how because I just watched some shots go by as I said to myself, "I am not getting that one tonight!" Little did I know that it would be my last time playing competitive tennis for some time, if ever again. My playing days were now permanently on the side lines until I could figure out what was wrong with the Brian Campkin Express, as I liked to call myself on the tennis court.

On Mar., 2nd, I went in for my stress test. I was really expecting it to be the answer and finally solve all my problems. I was under too much stress - stress that I had never felt before. I was, however, quite surprised at just how serious they were taking the whole procedure. I figured that

I would just start off by walking slowly, then go at a brisk pace until I was doing a light jog. I was very alarmed when the attending physician wanted to stay in the room with the technician as I did my test. I was under the impression that my doctor would be seeing me after the test to explain everything to me.

For the test, I was asked to walk at three minute intervals and then, the treadmill would speed up and tilt on an incline. The doctor also wanted me to alert them of any shortness of breath or pain that I might be experiencing, no matter how slight. At first, I was fine and smiling as I planned to beat the treadmill and the test. But as I approached my third interval, I was starting to feel like I did when I was on the tennis court chasing down a point. When I told the doctor that this is how I felt on the tennis courts, they immediately shut down the treadmill and pulled me off. I wasn't very encouraged by this to say the least. I had lost the battle with the treadmill and felt defeated. The shortness of breath was clearly not stress related.

A week later, which just happened to be the 16th anniversary of my Dad's death, I went to the doctor for my test results. At the time, I didn't know just how much the significance of my Dad's death was going to impact my own circumstances. The doctor seemed fairly calm, casual and at ease when he came into the room, however, when he started to speak about my stress test results, his whole demeanour changed and became very serious. He said that the stress test confirmed the positive results from the EKG.

That is when he told me that I needed yet another test. Boy, how many of these was I going to have to do before we knew what the heck was going on in my body? This whole thing was really testing my patience now! He started telling me that this time, I would be going to the local hospital for what is known as a MIBI test. He prescribed a cholesterol lowering drug, a blood pressure medication and told me to start taking 81mg of ASA.

Then, he dropped a bomb on me - he wanted me to fill a prescription for nitro glycerine spray. Now that scared the dickens out of me. Why did I need a spray to use in case I was having a heart attack? Where was this diagnosis trail taking me now? I was in a state of absolute shock.

This was the first time we zoned in on the heart and my pending troubles. Once I came out of my state of shock and was thinking a bit clearer, I realized that for the first time, we were dealing with something very serious here; it was my heart.

A MIBI test is basically an advanced stress test where and I.V. is hooked up to your arm and the MIBI, or radioactive fluid, is injected into your system. It's really weird as you would think that you would feel the fluid, but I never felt a thing. You then wait 30 minutes until the fluid circulates your body. A special camera then takes pictures of your heart at rest and then, you'll exercise by walking on a treadmill just like a regular stress test. Your blood pressure is also taken many times during this part of the test. Once the exercise is done, you lay down and have more pictures of your heart taken. This all seemed fairly clear to me, but I couldn't help but think that this was all about heart disease. I thought that I was too young and fit for this to be my outcome; this was something someone older and out of shape should be expecting. I just couldn't let go of the tight grasp on my internal denial dialogue.

On Thursday, March 15, I went to the hospital for my MIBI test that was scheduled for 8:30am. Once again, I set my sights on beating the treadmill and getting back to my normal healthy lifestyle, albeit everything I had been through, I had to admit that I was somewhat cautiously optimistic. Having the knowledge I gained from my research, I asked quite a few questions about the test, the process and how the results were going to be managed. I was told by the attending technician that if it wasn't too serious, for someone my age, I was likely to hear from my doctor in a few days. I also inquired what the expectations were of me on the treadmill. I was told that they needed a minimum of one minute's notice before I would need them to get me off of the treadmill because the dye needed that time to work through my system while I was at my peak position of fatigue. They stated that if I could get my heart rate up to 186 beats per minute that would be great. I now set my goal to beat the treadmill and deny any further talk about heart related issues for Brian Campkin!

The day was going fine albeit long and tedious until I finally got to jump up on the treadmill. One technician was monitoring the EKG and taking my blood pressure while the other was at the ready to inject the MIBI dye into the intravenous line. I was just trotting along fine and had reached the 8 minute mark when the EKG technician yelled to the other one, "Now!" She bolted out of her chair and injected the dye and at exactly one minute, they shut me down and got me off of the treadmill. I thought, "Damn it, I didn't even make the 9 minute mark again!" What was this going to mean for me now on this extensive test?

From there, I had to rest for eight minutes so they could get my heart rate down before they took the second set of pictures. Those few minutes seemed like an eternity as all kinds of erratic and scary thoughts filled my head. At one point, I remember thinking, "Geez do I need a heart transplant or something? I must because I never had a heart attack, just shortness of breath!" From that moment on, I was no longer on the destination to denial; I landed firmly on reality road.

After they took the pictures, I assumed that my wife, Lori, and I would leave the hospital to await our results mid to early next week as the nurse had told me earlier in the day. But after the attending doctor saw my preliminary results, he said that my photos were being processed as a rush so that the on staff cardiologist could review them with me. The first thing he said was that what they saw was serious and then, he took me into his little examination room and asked me some general health and family history questions, while conducting a blood pressure test.

He then sat my wife and me across his desk and stated that he wanted me to immediately go in for an angiogram. He began calling around the hospital as we stared at him wondering what the heck an angiogram was. It was now 3 o'clock in the afternoon and we had spent the better part of a day on this MIBI test and now, he was telling me that they wanted to shove a camera up the artery in my groin to take pictures of my heart. For goodness sake, when was all this insanity going to stop? When was I going to wake up and realize that I was only dreaming? And then I thought, if only that was true!

As the doctor spoke, I thought to myself, "I was having shortness of breath five weeks ago and now these so called experts are talking about heart disease, clogged arteries and by-pass surgery." That last word snapped me back into the room as the doctor laid out what lies ahead and how this test would be a clear indication of what I was truly dealing with. I held onto those words and felt some solace in the fact that we were coming to the end. But geez, I'm only 46 years old and too young for this! This was my last gasp and grasp at denial, I was done.

After the doctor finished explaining the procedure to us, he explained that the hospital unfortunately did not have a bed for me on the cardiology floor so I would have to come back the next day, March 16th, Julie, my middle daughter's 17th birthday. How's that for a fine birthday present? Here you go honey, a sick Dad for you. Wow, I was really bitter now.

After a restless night's sleep, Lori and I headed to the hospital. This procedure involves inserting a long thin tube called a catheter into an artery at the top of your leg or groin area, which was done with the use of a local freezing. The tip of the catheter is gently guided through the artery to the heart under x-ray vision. They say that the test isn't painful and that the catheter is removed as soon as the test has been completed. On average, this test can last for about 40 minutes and is surprisingly a comfortable and uneventful procedure. The only scary statistic is that there is a 1 in 1000 chance of a heart attack, stroke or death taking place during the procedure. That last piece of information scared me a little bit, but when I looked at my age and excellent health, I wasn't too concerned.

I was eager to finally get the results of my test and move on with this impeding health challenge.

We arrived at the hospital that morning and they quickly got me into a gown and bed. At a quick glance, it appeared that my bed was fifth in line, so it was going to be a couple hours wait for sure. In the meantime, the nurse assigned to me came over and got me all prepped by taking some blood, putting in an I.V. and reviewing the full procedure with me. Oh, and then the uncomfortable part of being shaved below the waist. I wasn't told to have this pre-done before arriving, which was a little embarrassing to say the least. To pass the time, Lori and I took turns reading all of the pamphlets given to us on heart disease, by-pass surgery, fat free diets and many other related topics.

Finally, it was my turn. They wheeled me to the operating room and got up on the table. The cardiologist explained the procedure to me again as they froze and got me settled in. It was kind of weird to be awake during this whole thing, but I thought to myself, "Let the games begin and let's finally move forward!" They were right. The procedure was fairly comfortable, well, as comfortable as it can be to have a tiny camera placed up your groin and into your chest. I could feel the tube going in and traveling up to my chest, but I didn't experience any pain.

Once the tube was in place, the doctor injected the dye that would show up on the X-ray and show the effects of the pumping chambers of the heart and the blood vessels that supply blood to the heart muscle. I could actually feel the warm sensation of the dye going to my heart, which was freaky, and see most of the procedure on the monitor, which was kind of cool.

When they were done, the doctor removed the tube and applied immediate pressure to my incision in my groin. Before going back to my bed, the doctor explained the blockages I had. He might as well have spoken in some foreign language; all I heard him say was, "You will need by-pass surgery Mr. Campkin!" Holy cow! Five weeks of testing and an angiogram later, I had heart disease and required a triple by-pass. I'm only 46 years old; this is an old person's disease. I had shortness of breath playing tennis. This shouldn't be the outcome I had to deal with; life should have dealt me a much different hand for sure. I immediately started to wonder what my long term side effects and implications were going to be. I had so many unanswered questions and so many questions that I had not even thought of yet.

Then I thought, "Wow, how am I going to explain this to Lori" as she waited in the original room that I was prepped in. Then, one of the nurses wheeled me back to my bed and asked, "Do you want to tell your wife or should I?" Since I didn't really hear what the doctor had said to me in the operating room, I told her to go ahead. She was probably more experienced in delivering this type of news than I was. Boy was I wrong. She blurted out to Lori, "Well it's a triple by-pass at a minimum, now lay still Mr. Campkin and your nurse will tend to you shortly." Geez, whatever happened to bedside manner? Lori went immediately into shock, laid her head on my chest and started to sob. I remember telling her not to worry; I was young, strong and ready to take this on, but I don't think she heard a single word I said.

Finally, my nurse came by and put a clamp on the incision in my groin so she could cauterize it. Then, a hospital volunteer came over and spoke to us about the pending procedure, gave us a number of pamphlets from the Heart and Stroke Foundation and St. Michael's Hospital. This lady was great at explaining everything to us and even told us about hotels close to the hospital. She even shared a brief story on being a survivor of heart disease herself, which was a little comforting for us both. In the end, we were chatting casually and sharing a few laughs, which seemed to be a good stress release. What I didn't know was that laughing wasn't good for my incision; I started to hemorrhage. The other nurse came running over and began putting her full weight on my groin to stop the internal bleeding for 15 minutes - man, did that hurt. I just grimaced, squeezed her arm and clenched my teeth. I thought that open heart surgery had to be less painful than this procedure.

Once the bleeding stopped, she scolded me to lie still so that I could recover properly and go home. I did exactly what she said for the balance of the afternoon and finally, around 4:30pm, we were sent home. Over the next few days, the bruising started to settle in nicely; I had a purple and yellow bruise just above my knee to below my waist. It actually took a couple of weeks before the pain in my groin was gone completely. As we drove home, however, both Lori and I rode in silence. I think we were both thinking the same thing, "How were we going to tell our three daughters that I needed to have open heart surgery?"

Julie's 17th Birthday with her cousins Bryanne and Dayne

Rouge Valley Hospital where I had my angiogram and
attended my cardiac rehabilliatation program

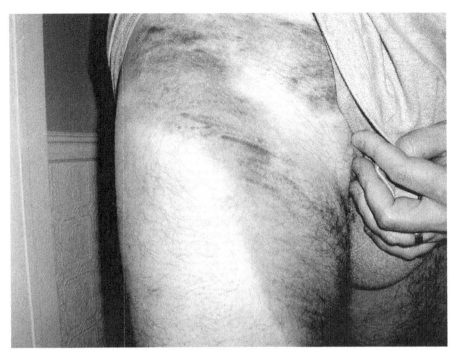

The evidence of my bad behaviour post angiogram and the bad bruising I had

Teddy Bear for the hospital from my girls

Cumin and Cilantro Bean

Ingredients
1 can (19 oz/540 mL) white kidney beans, drained and rinsed
2 Tbsp (25 mL) canola oil
2 Tbsp (25 mL) balsamic vinegar
1 tsp (5 mL) cumin
1 clove garlic, minced
¼ tsp (1 mL) crushed red pepper flakes
1 Tbsp (15 mL) chopped fresh cilantro
3 Tbsp (45 mL) finely chopped red onion
1 tsp (5 mL) lime zest
¼ tsp (1 mL) pepper

Directions

In a blender or food processor, combine all ingredients. Blend or pulse to desired consistency. Transfer mixture to a container. Cover and refrigerate for 2–3 hours to allow flavours to develop. Makes 8 servings.

Nutritional analysis - per serving (2 Tbsp/25 mL)
Calories: 35
Protein: 2 g
Total Fat: 1.5 g
Saturated Fat: 0 g
Cholesterol: 0 mg
Carbohydrates: 4 g
Fibre: 2 g
Sodium: 0 mg

Recipes from the Quick and Healthy Cookbook developed by The Heart and Stroke Foundation and Manitoba Canola Growers Association

Chapter 3 – How Will My Children React?

"The secret of man's being is not only to live but to have something to live for."

~ Fyodor Dostoevsky, Russian Novelist, 1821 – 1881.

The moment the doctor uttered those words, "Mr. Campkin you're going to need by-pass surgery!" I immediately set a life goal for myself. I decided that although this diagnosis had set me back, it wasn't going to keep me down forever, if at all. I set a goal for myself that I wanted to be healthy enough to walk my three teenage daughters down the aisle when their wedding days arrived. I also decided that a positive attitude was one of the best allies that I could have right now. These goals were set thanks to a statistic I read in one of the pamphlets from the Heart and Stroke Foundation. It said, "that 50% of people, who are first diagnosed with heart disease, their first symptom is death." I totally related to this; it reminded me about the difference between my Dad and me.

It was living proof for me. The statistic was very accurate and I was very fortunate to have been provided an awesome second chance at life. It was this renowned positive outlook on life that my wife and I embarked on telling our kids at dinner that night about my "situation" as we came to call it. My kids knew that Lori and I had been at the hospital all day and that we were hoping to be home in time for Julie's birthday dinner that night. They were expecting an update from us, but not this.

Before we had dinner, we sat the kids down and explained the day's event and what had transpired. We let them know that at the end of our story, I had been diagnosed with a serious illness where three of my main arteries were almost 100% clogged; I would have to go back to the hospital as soon as I confirm an appointment with the Chief of Cardiology at St. Michaels Hospital. They were going to open up my chest and work on my clogged arteries so that I could breathe normally once again and resume a normal life.

We explained in lay terms of what they could expect now that their dad was sick. We spoke truthfully and let them know that I was going to be fine - this surgery is done all the time. We informed them how long we thought that I would be in the hospital based on the facts that have been presented to us so far. They would be able to come visit me once I was out of the intensive care unit. We also warned them that I would look a little sore and would have a long healing process. Thus, I would not be doing any heavy lifting or running, but I will be accepting all the "gentle" hugs that I could get.

Megan, my eldest, who was 19 and in her first year of University, fully understood the situation, but was shocked. Julie, my middle daughter, who was turning 17 that very day, understood but was confused. Kelly, my youngest, who was 13 and in grade 8, really didn't understand what was going on and asked her older sister for some clarification, which helped somewhat.

Later that evening, I decided to sit with Kelly to give her a better understanding. I started off by referring to her favourite movie, The Wizard of Oz. I said, "I want you to look at me as the Tin Man. My heart is broken and I have to go see a wizard, or in this case, a heart surgeon to fix me up. It's not in Emerald City though; it is at hospital called St. Mike's. Does this make sense to you Kelly?" She replied, "Sure Dad. I get it now. This doctor is going to cut you open and move all sorts of parts around to make you better, right?" "Exactly," I replied. Then, she said, "Great, can I go play now?" From this moment on, Tin Man became my nickname.

A year later, I asked my daughters to write down their reactions to my heart surgery. Here are their stories.

My youngest, Kelly

The moment I found out my dad had to go in for bypass surgery, I really did not understand what was going on. My Aunt Debbie and family were in our living room a few days after finding out the news and they were busy preparing a list of family and friends to call and tell them about this sad news. It was at this point; I turned to my sister, Megan, and asked her, "Why is this such a big deal?" My sister turned to me a said, "Dad's going to have surgery that can be very dangerous Kelly that is why this is such a big deal!"

After that moment, every day I learned a bit more and started to understand what was going on, as this became a common topic in our house. My sisters took it more seriously than I did the first month or so because I never fully wrapped my head around the fact that my dad would be getting cut open and moving all sorts of things around in his body to try to fix him.

My family and I started watching Grey's Anatomy a few months before the surgery, everyone except my dad that is. It seemed like in every episode at least one person would die or barely survive. As I got into this show and saw more loved ones dying, I started to thinking, "What if I lose the man who has always been there for me?" He was there to motivate me at 6 a.m. for hockey practice, coached me as only a good father can to be a better baseball player and always gave me the confidence to sing or perform in front of family and friends.

What if I lost my dad, the person who made me who I am today? Where would I be now? All this was answered the day my mom and sister Megan took my dad to the hospital for his surgery. When they called to say his surgery was over and he was OK, all my worries and fears lifted from my heart and mind as the person I thought was going to be lost was given a second chance at life.

My second child, Julie

I'll never forget the day I found out that my dad had heart disease: it was my 17th birthday. I didn't understand why God gave me a sick dad for a birthday gift. My family had never been faced with a tragedy like this before. However, I soon realized why God gave us, as a family, an obstacle to overcome. It is because I have a loving family, who is strong and very close; there was no way we were going to let this bring us down. Through hope and support, my dad had a very successful surgery. His heart is still going strong today to prove it. Throughout this whole ordeal, I never lost faith in my family, in God and especially, in my dad.

He is very strong and determined man, who had the right mindset, and he never let his sickness bring him down. Instead, it made him an even healthier, happier person. I am thankful to this day that my family is stronger than ever and sometimes all it takes is a little faith.

My eldest, Megan

I remember the day that I found out my dad needed to have triple bypass surgery. It was quite the process to get to this point. It was winter and the whole family had been sick with colds. So when he was tired and out of breath from playing tennis, we thought he was still fighting off his cold. However, the cold just wouldn't go away and he knew there was something more, so he went to his doctor. They ran tests and saw nothing wrong, yet he was still tiring out easily. He was persistent with his doctor, however, and wanted to find out what was causing this. I am very glad my dad was determined to find an answer because there is no way he would have been walking around for very long.

When my mom told me after a long day of tests that my dad had three clogged arteries, I was shocked. He didn't smoke, wasn't overweight, exercised and ate pretty well, so I didn't understand how this came out of nowhere. I was upset and scared because any surgery has risks, but heart surgery is definitely not something to be taken lightly. As a family, we came to terms with the diagnosis and got ready for dad to go for surgery.

I think the hardest part was the wait that followed my dad being diagnosed. It felt like, at any point, something could happen like a heart attack. At this point, his heart was not damaged at all, which was very good news, but that did not mean that damage could not be done. His surgery was pushed three weeks and then, they called to push it again. This was very frustrating; we all just wanted it to be over so he could be back at home recovering. Finally the day came; it was my last exam for my first year at university and my dad's surgery all at the same time.

Luckily, the hospital was a five-minute walk from my school, so I joined my mom and dad on our early trip to the hospital. It felt like there was a lot of waiting for him to go into the operating room. I had mixed feelings because I wanted it to be over, but I also didn't want to see him being rolled away. The actual waiting during his surgery was not as long as I thought it would be. I had to leave and write my exam at one point, which probably helped to break up the wait. I made it back in time to hear that it had gone really well and dad was in recovery. I was very, very happy and relieved.

I know that bypass surgery is very routine and common, but when it is being done on someone you are very close to, whom you love, then it doesn't feel so common and routine. I am glad my dad was given a second chance and that he took full advantage of it. He has recovered very well and has followed his rehab religiously. I am very proud of him.

As you can see, I had three very special reasons for setting my "life goal" of walking my daughters down the aisle on their wedding day. I was going to do everything in my power to ensure that they were provided more and more Dad time after my surgery. I knew that it was all going to start with me having a positive outcome on my journey.

Family photo a couple years after my surgery

Julie, Megan and Kelly with my Mom on one of our many visits to her apartment and pool

Kelly and I a couple of years after my surgery. I am wearing my first Ride for Heart shirt

My girls on our Mexico vacation just before my diagnosis

The girls the year after my surgery in 2008

Photo of Julie, Kelly and Megan for some Heart and Stroke volunteering

The girls age 1, 4 and 6 in 1994

The girls age 1, 4 and 6 after Kelly's bath

My 3 young ladies all grown up

The girls on halloween in 1995

Mango Quinoa Salad

Ingredients
2 cups (500 mL) cooked quinoa, cooled
¼ cup (50 mL) dried cranberries
2 (~1 cup) (2, apx 250 mL) mango, finely chopped
½ English cucumber, chopped
½ red pepper, chopped
2 green onions, chopped
2 Tbsp (25 mL) slivered almonds
2 Tbsp (25 mL) chopped fresh flat leaf parsley
2 Tbsp (25 mL) canola oil
1 Tbsp (15 mL) white wine vinegar
1 juice of an orange
1 Tbsp (15 mL) grated orange zest

¼ tsp (1 mL) pepper
½ tsp (2 mL) cumin
½ tsp (2 mL) granulated sugar

Directions
Place quinoa in a medium-sized serving bowl. Add, cranberries, mango, cucumber, red pepper, green onions, almonds and parsley to the quinoa. In a salad dressing container combine canola oil, white wine vinegar, orange juice and zest, pepper, cumin and sugar. Shake vigorously and set aside. Pour dressing over top and toss salad to coat with the dressing. Makes 6 servings.

Nutritional analysis - per serving (about 3/4 cup/175 mL)
Calories: 200
Protein: 4 g
Total Fat: 7 g
Saturated Fat: 0.5 g
Cholesterol: 0 mg
Carbohydrates: 32 g
Fibre: 3 g
Sodium: 0 mg

Recipes from the Quick and Healthy Cookbook developed by The Heart and Stroke Foundation and Manitoba Canola Growers Association

Chapter 4 – Attitude is Everything

"A strong positive mental attitude will create more miracles than any wonder drug."

~ Patricia Neal
American Actress, 1926 – 2010.

have always been a very positive person; I always see the glass as half full. I'm not sure if this was because I became a huge Toronto Maple Leaf NHL hockey fan in 1968, the year after they won their last Stanley Cup, and shared the championship drought with them since then or if it's just who I am. However, I do know that heart disease has tested my ability to keeping a positive attitude.

I'm sure that we have all heard the saying, *"It's not what happens to you, it's how you handle it that counts."* Well, this became my rallying cry when I left Centenary Hospital on March 16th with news that I was going to require open-heart surgery. I believe that I did three key things after my diagnosis that led to a successful surgery and recovery. The first thing I did was to search the internet for positive, motivational and uplifting quotes. Now, I know that it sounds corny or downright silly, but I took a business course a few years ago, where they spoke about how inspiration brings motivation and a desire to succeed. If you think about it, you will likely recall a moment in your life when you got inspired and had a strong desire to take on a challenge, event or activity with a renewed vigour. This was exactly how I wanted to take on my journey with heart disease.

I also had three teenage daughters and a wife worrying about me. I thought that if I had a good attitude towards this whole ordeal, then they would hopefully follow suit. In fact, whenever I engaged in a conversation, I always lead with the fact that this was an awesome second chance for me and that I was going to take advantage of it. I think that this strategy really worked and helped put my family at ease. With that being said, I don't want you to think that I was walking around in a state of bliss or looking at life through rose coloured glasses. Truth be told that deep down, I was terrified. I had no idea what the future held for me, but I figured that my fear was all about having something to lose, which is entirely normal and natural.

But as I searched for daily quotes and posted it to my Facebook page, it gave me a sense of warmth, hope and understanding. In fact, a year after my surgery, I stopped posting quotes on my Facebook page for a day or two because I felt that I did not need them anymore. What happened afterwards astounded me. I was inundated with notes and messages from my FB friends requesting that I continue posting quotes - they needed and read them every day. Wow, I had no idea that my goal in helping myself actually helped others. I can't tell you how good that made me feel. And yes, I still post my quotes to this day for all to see and benefit from in their own way.

The other key strategy I took on with my positive attitude was that I never complained. From the moment I was diagnosed until my surgery date, I went about my daily life quietly. If I had to use one word to describe my true feelings, it would be "anxious." It was very difficult to be walking around knowing that I had three extremely clogged arteries that might make me keel over at any moment.

In fact, I remember Lori asking me one day to make a trip to the basement to grab a loaf of bread out of freezer for lunch. I looked at her and immediately declined her request. She thought that I was kidding and shrugged it off with a snicker and repeated her question. I graciously declined once again. Then, she got stern with me and asked why I wouldn't help her with lunch by getting a loaf from the freezer. When I explained to her that I didn't know if taking the stairs might kill me - I was serious. She put her head down and went to get the bread. This is how I felt; I stayed positive and wasn't complaining. I was also being realistic in what I was dealing with as I awaited my surgery date.

A phone call from my family doctor later put me at ease. I joked that I didn't think doctors still made house calls. He laughed and then, got serious when he asked how I was doing. I expressed my fear of walking around with heart disease. He told me to use common sense and to not do anything ridiculous, such as raking leaves or shoveling snow. When I told him that I watched my wife rake this past weekend, he laughed again. After I hung up, I felt better about this whole ordeal. My doctor somehow knew how to calm me down. The fact that he took time out of his busy schedule to call me was, well, very special. I will never forget him for doing that.

The last thing that helped put my mind and body at ease was that we got a puppy. Now, I don't want you to think that everyone, who gets diagnosed with heart disease, should get a new pet, but having our new Shih Tzu around was amazing. I also knew that getting Lori on board was going to test my selling skills, which I had developed over the past dozen years in my role in the Information Technology sector.

So with that in mind, I remembered hearing that having a pet can have health benefits and can be very therapeutic. As I had done with my forthcoming surgery, I did a lot of research on this topic to support my case. What I found was more than what I had bargained for. One article stated that the average domestic pet - dog, cat or even a fish - can provide many health benefits. Pets can actually ease loneliness, reduce stress, encourage exercise and provide unconditional love and affection. I found my wining sales pitch.

The article went on to say that studies also found that:

→ Pet owners are less likely to suffer from depression than those without pets.

→ People with pets have lower blood pressure in stressful situations than those without pets.

→ Playing with a pet can elevate levels of serotonin and dopamine, which can calm and relax.

→ Pet owners have lower triglyceride and cholesterol levels (indicators of heart disease) than those without pets.

→ Heart attack patients with pets survive longer than those without.

→ Pet owners over age 65 make fewer visits to their doctors than those without pets.

→ While people with dogs often experience the greatest health benefits, a pet doesn't necessarily have to be a dog or a cat. Even watching a fish in an aquarium can help reduce muscle tension and lower pulse rate.

After I shared all of the benefits of a pet with Lori, especially statistics for heart attack patients, lowering blood pressure and stress, she was instantly on board. I don't think a doctor could have written a better prescription for getting a pet.

On Sunday, we drove 25 minutes into the country to a small town just north of our home in Whitby to see the breeder. We were looking at a few new puppies until Julie held up this little brown and white furry pup. Within minutes, we all fell in love with him and made an instant decision about our new family member. We asked the breeder if the puppy was actually available. He smiled broadly and said that he was all ours! We did a family-group hug right there in the breeders barn and named our new pup Jackson.

At the end of the day, I can't put enough emphasis on how my attitude was the key difference for me to set myself up for a good bypass surgery experience. I truly believe that having a positive outlook allowed me to have such a miraculous recovery. Having Jackson and his outgoing personality around brought immediate joy to our home. It was great for me to have him around as the rest of the family went about their daily routines of work, school and homework. I had no idea how much he was going to contribute to my recovery. As we know, all dogs need to be walked!

With my personal recovery trainer Jackson days after my surgery

The breeders place where we bought Jackson

Baby Jackson first days home

Baby Jackson first days home with Julie

Baby Jackson first days home

The day we picked out Jackson from the breeders

Jackson's first Christmas December 2007

Moroccan Pulse Salad

Salad Ingredients
1 can (19 oz/540 mL) lentils, drained and rinsed
1 can (19 oz/540 mL) chickpeas, drained and rinsed
3 green onions, chopped
1 red pepper, seeded and diced
1 green pepper, seeded and diced
1 jalapeno pepper, seeded and diced
2 tsp (10 mL) orange zest
1 orange, peeled and cut into segments
¼ cup (50 mL) slivered almonds, toasted
½ cup (125 mL) dried cranberries
¼ cup (50 mL) slivered dried apricots

Dressing Ingredients
1/4 cup (50 mL) canola oil
2 Tbsp (25 mL) lemon juice
½ tsp (2 mL) cumin
½ tsp (2 mL) ground coriander
1/8 tsp (0.5 mL) cayenne pepper
1/8 tsp (0.5 mL) black pepper

Combine all salad ingredients in large salad bowl. In a small bowl, whisk together dressing ingredients. Add dressing and mix to combine. Makes 10 servings.

Nutritional analysis - per serving
Calories: 260
Protein: 11 g
Fat: 9 g
Saturated fat: 0.5 g
Cholesterol: 0 mg
Carbohydrates: 38 g
Fibre: 10 g
Sodium: 5 mg

Recipes from the Quick and Healthy Cookbook developed by The Heart and Stroke Foundation and Manitoba Canola Growers Association

Chapter 5 – The Waiting Game

"No pain that we suffer, no trial that we experience is wasted. It ministers to our education, to the development of such qualities as patience, faith, fortitude and humility. All that we suffer and all that we endure, especially when we endure it patiently, builds up our characters, purifies our hearts, expands our souls, and makes us more tender and charitable, more worthy to be called the children of God . . . and it is through sorrow and suffering, toil and tribulation, that we gain the education that we come here to acquire and which will make us more like our Father and Mother in heaven."

- Orson F. Whitney
Journalist and Poet, 1855 – 1931.

When people ask me what the hardest part in my journey with heart disease was, I always say, "It was the waiting game". It took six weeks for my surgery date. During that time, there were a few things that stood out the most for me during my waiting game.

First, my body felt like a house in the middle of the night. You know when you lay awake at night you can hear every creak and squeak the house makes. Well, my body felt the same way. I was definitely more acutely aware of every ping and pang that my body was making.

Sure enough, one day I was just lounging around the house when I felt this odd sensation in my chest, it only lasted about a half hour; so I let it go. However, when it re-occurred at lunch time for another half hour, I mentioned it to my wife and we immediately went to the hospital, just as my doctor had urged me to.

When we arrived at the emergency department check-in, they took my health card. Before they could ask any questions, I told them that I was a triple by-pass candidate waiting for my surgery date and had had some chest pains that morning. They immediately checked me into a bed and began the procedure by inserting me with an I.V., taking some blood work, hooking me up to a heart monitor and taking chest X-rays right at my bedside. I figured that it was so I couldn't move around or get up and put any stress on my heart. It took about 15 minutes to do from the moment I entered the hospital. I felt like a celebrity with V.I.P. service, but then I remembered that I was in a hospital, not a five star resort.

I was hoping that the rest of the testing would go quickly and painlessly. However, when I asked the on staff cardiologist how long the testing would take, I was told that the procedure required blood work four to five hours apart in order to see if there was any stress related activity on my heart. All I could think was, "damn, this may put me at risk for missing the Maple Leaf hockey game that night on T.V. and they were fighting once again to try to make the playoffs." I told my nurses to speed it up if they could so that I could see the game; they just chuckled and called me, "high maintenance!" We all smiled and I settled in for the balance of the afternoon and awaited the results.

Lori and I decided that she might as well take off and get home to feed the girls, who would all be coming home from school. She agreed and said that we would eat when I got home. She came back shortly after dinner to see me eating a low-fat meal from the hospital and grumbled because she thought that I was going to wait for her to eat. I excused my actions with a quick, "I do have heart disease you know and I was famished." She smiled and said that she understood. We settled in to wait for the results by playing a few games of cards. Shortly after my dinner, they came in to tell me that my results were fine and that I could go home. I was really happy to hear good news. Now I understood what some of my pings and pangs really were. The uneasiness I felt in my chest was just the routine method of my body working each day. Oh, and I was home just in time for the puck drop for the Leafs game. Life was good - first, a positive outcome on my test results and now, hopefully a Leafs victory.

The Leafs did win that night, but unfortunately they didn't finish strong the following week and were out of the playoffs for another year. In hindsight, I think the outcome might have been best for my heart. After all, I tend to take hockey seriously and not having a team to cheer for this particular year was most likely a good thing for my stress level.

After the incident took place, I was fortunate to have a number of family and friends reach out to me to see if I was up to take on company. After being home for a few weeks on my own during the day, it was a very welcoming invitation. I had past work colleagues invite me out to a lunch to catch up and renew friendships. I had current work colleagues come visit, who try their best not to bring up any work related stories or topics for the fear of causing me any stress. I actually enjoyed watching them do this because it was quite entertaining for me. I had guys from my old hockey team take me out to a pub, where I got to watch them order a burger, fries and beer as I chowed down on some fish, salad and ice water. Boy, how things had already changed for me.

I really enjoyed when my best buddy Ken called to see if he could come out and spend the afternoon with me. He is a firefighter and it was his day off so it worked out well for both of us. He was going to help me "Jackson-proof" our back yard so that the new pup couldn't find his way out and have scavenger hunts in our neighbor's yards. Afterwards, we went out for a bite to eat and then came back to play some board games. He also downloaded some computer games for me to play during my recovery - he felt that my mobility would be jeopardized and this would be a good way for me to pass the time while taking comfort in my bed. While the games were downloading, we played a few games of Scrabble and whiled the afternoon away with some small talk. Neither one of us really wanted to dive into a deep conversation about what I was going through, but we could see in each other's eyes how concerned we were. I really can't put a price on what his visit and the others meant to me.

On the Saturday of Easter weekend, I was watching some hockey when the phone rang. It was my eldest sister, Debbie, calling to tell me that my good friend, Mike, had just passed away from a massive heart attack! I was totally stunned, shocked and silent. I just kept thinking why was I given so many warnings and yet Mike, just like my Dad, was taken without having this privilege.

I went back downstairs to the T.V., but I never really saw or heard any of the hockey game. I just kept thinking and asking myself questions like, how could Mike be dead? Why him? Why not me? Why did I get this second chance? And what could I possibly do to prove that I was actually worthy of this second chance? How could I ever overcome this guilt? I fell asleep that night with these thoughts echoing in my mind.

A couple of days later, we attended Mike's funeral and I have to say that it was the hardest funeral I had ever attended. It was more difficult than my Dad's, Mom's or even my grandparents. Sitting in that church pew was so surreal. I kept having thoughts of guilt and could not get over how I was waiting to have my heart surgery so that I could get back to having a normal, healthy life, whereas Mike's just ended at the age of 48 without any warning. I finally decided that I better listen to my body and just let my emotions flow as I began having trouble breathing. I watched

Joanie's brother-in-law, who is a minister, deliver a beautiful service and tribute in Mike's honour. But when Joanie's nephew began singing, I lost it. Tears just rolled down my cheeks and I let them; it felt good to release all of my emotions at church.

The balance of my waiting game was rather uneventful. I spent many hours doing something I had not done for some time, which was some recreational reading. Prior to my diagnosis, I spent most of my reading time on personal development books. I took this "down time" to lose myself into somebody else's life. The author I dove into was James Patterson - who my daughter Julie introduced me to. I must have devoured about four or five of his great mystery novels. I was also fairly strict with my social calendar because I didn't want to get rundown before my surgery, but I did appreciate everyone reaching out to me.

All in all, I went through many different emotions during my waiting game. I believe the one thing that helped me get through it was the awesome support and guidance I received from my family, friends, colleagues and doctors. Without their unconditional support, I know that my waiting game would have been a much more trying time for me.

With my best buddy Ken

One of the last photo's I had with my good buddy Mike Fox

Lori with our good friends Scott and Marie along with Jackson and their two dogs Angie and Frankie

Jackson and I spending one of our many afternoons chilling in the living room waiting for my surgery

Mike with Joanie and her two girls, Sheree and Kirsten

Mike and I pitching horseshoes at one of the many August long weekends we spent together

Lemon Roasted Potatoes

Tip: For an extra crisp on your potatoes, heat the pan in the oven and add the potatoes to the hot cookie sheet. The skin will have an extra crunch. Remember, eating the skin of your potatoes increases the nutrient content and fibre in your meal.

Ingredients
1 ½ lbs (750 g) mini red potatoes, cut in half lengthwise
2 tsp (10 mL) canola oil
1 large clove garlic, minced
1 tsp (5 mL) dried rosemary, crushed
2 tsp (10 mL) grated lemon zest
2 Tbsp (25 mL) lemon juice
½ tsp (2 mL) paprika
¼ tsp (1 mL) freshly ground black pepper

Directions

Preheat oven to 425°F (220 C). In a large bowl, combine pota-toes, canola oil, garlic, rosemary, lemon zest and juice, paprika and pepper; toss until potatoes are well coated. Spread potatoes onto

a parchment paper lined roasting pan and roast for 45 minutes, stirring occasionally until golden brown and tender. Makes 4 servings.

Nutrition Facts: per serving (¾ cup/175 mL)
Calories: 190
Protein: 5 g
Total Fat: 2.5 g
Saturated Fat: 0 g
Cholesterol: 0 mg
Carbohydrates: 38 g
Fibre: 4 g
Sodium: 20 mg

Recipes from the Quick and Healthy Cookbook developed by The Heart and Stroke Foundation and Manitoba Canola Growers Association

Chapter 6 – My R & D – Research and Delays

The difference between school and life? In school, you're taught a lesson and then given a test. In life, you're given a test that teaches you a lesson.

- Tom Bodett
American Actor, born 1955.

Once I got over the shock of being a healthy 46-year-old, who had just been diagnosed with heart disease, I realized just how little I knew about my heart. I was obviously aware of heart attacks and strokes, but I had always related them to older people and certainly not to me. I decided that I needed to go back to school in a manner of speaking. I needed to take the time to educate myself on the journey that lies ahead for my family and me. I always believed that knowledge is power and I knew that if I could get an understanding of heart disease, I could deal with it better.

I remember that shortly after the cardiologist dropped this bomb on us, I was living life in fear and confusion. With that in mind, I got up early one morning and decided to surf the net. I started with the Heart and Stroke Canada website and found many items and articles that were quite useful. I also tripped across a section on volunteering as a survivor speaker. I immediately had a bright idea. This was my calling. This is why I had been given a second chance and my friend Mike and my Dad had not. Without a moment's hesitation, I picked up the phone and called the foundation.

A lady answered after two rings and asked if she could help me. With tremendous passion and enthusiasm, I told her about my desire to be a survivor speaker. She was very excited and began asking me a few questions like, "What was your heart incident?" "When did it happen?" "How are you feeling today?" When I responded with, "I am scheduled to have a triple by-pass, but the date is not confirmed and I have not hit recovery road yet." She paused and then said, "Well Mr. Campkin, perhaps we should wait until you get all that behind you first and then we can chat more." I hung up the phone a little disappointed, but couldn't help but think that she was right. They need me to be a survivor before they can engage with me to be a survivor speaker, don't you think?

After I had a quick chuckle, I remembered that I had an armful of literature from the Heart and Stroke Foundation that I received when we left the hospital on that afternoon of my diagnosis. So I grabbed a coffee and settled in for a morning of reading. One booklet that I found to be absolutely amazing was called, "Recovery Road" from the Heart and Stroke. It told me everything from what to expect and informed me about my heart, my procedure, coming home, the recovery and beyond. I absorbed this booklet a few times; it really gave me clarity on what to expect before and after my surgery. I was nervous and anxious about having the procedure obviously - it's not easy to put your heart in the hands of a surgeon and his team. I was also really excited about the ball being back in my court and being on recovery road. It was my ultimate goal to just hear my heart beat and to be able to be back on my two feet.

The information I was provided with was great, but I wanted to know more, which was a great thing. I went back to the web and did some more surfing searching "heart disease", "bypass surgery" and "recovery from open heart surgery". I did promise myself, however, that I wouldn't do any research by viewing a video of the actual procedure. It was just a personal preference for me; I didn't want to see what I was going to go through. Reading about it was fine, but watching it, well, seeing wasn't believing for me this time around.

I also had many people approach me to say that they knew someone who had gone through the procedure and that they would be happy to set up a call for me. Although I appreciated their invitation, I was hesitant because I didn't want to have someone else's experience communicated to me - I wanted to have my own. I was trying to limit my knowledge to facts versus other people's opinions and experiences. I wasn't being self-ish; it was for me, just like someone telling you how you are going to react when you're being introduced to somebody for the first time. I wanted to make my own first impression. At the end of the day, I didn't want to hear anything negative or anything that may change or alter my positive outlook that I had created for myself. With that being said, I spoke to two individuals before my surgery.

My good friend, Scott, had his Dad call me without warning, so I really couldn't avoid the conversation. His Dad, Mel, had been through by-pass surgery; they thought it would be good if I had some first-hand knowledge on what to expect. Mel was very genuine and caring in shar-ing his experience with me and wanted me to know over and over again that it was his experience and my actual events may be different. He didn't really tell me anything that I didn't already read; he reinforced a lot for me.

He did say that if I was a shy person, the hospital stay would soon change that. He had a lot of people poking him, prodding him, bathing him, working around and cleaning his "Jimmy Johnson," as he put it. I howled when he told me because he delivered it in such a matter of fact and innocent way. Although, I could hear the awkwardness in his voice as if he was going through it all over again. We hung up and I thought how nice it was of him to call me since I had never met him before. I chuckled for days about the whole Jimmy Johnson thing.

The other call I got was from my sister-in-law's father, Ken, who had his heart surgery a week ago. I couldn't get over how great he sounded - we chatted for about a half hour. I just kept thinking, "Geez, I hope I sound this great right after my surgery." He provided me with a lot of guidance on what to expect and reassurance that even though it is open heart surgery, it's a smooth process. He shared a lot about his initial recovery and how much he started walking, which really blew me away and excited me about my own recovery expectations. He wished me good luck and we hung up the phone. Both conversations really helped me prepare and understand my upcoming surgery and put my mind at ease.

As you can see, I did a fair amount of research before my surgery. I truly believe that it had a direct impact on setting me up for a successful experience and recovery.

My next piece of research took place on Monday, April the 2nd when we finally went to St. Michael's Hospital to meet with my heart surgeon for a consult. We had to wait a bit to see him and as we waited, Lori asked me to go over to the wall in his waiting area and read what was on the enormous plaque. It was sent from China to thank St. Michael's hospital and their Chief of Cardiology for their contribution in training Chinese exchange students, who had come over for their education. I was really happy to see that my heart surgeon was actually the Chief of Cardiology. Wow, was I in good hands or what?

When we finally got to meet the doctor, he actually had two Chinese students in his office, which was cool to see the inscription on the plaque in action. Now that he had physically seen me, his first comment was that I looked too young to have this kind of surgery. This was a common theme for me. I did look too young to be having a triple by-pass, but unfortunately heart disease doesn't discriminate against you regardless of your age, gender or ethnic background. It just chooses you as it did with me. After our initial introductions, the doctor explained the procedure in great detail, which really reinforced everything that I had read.

The real interesting part was when he showed me the actual video of my heart from the angiogram. This was the first time I saw it up close and had it explained to me. He showed us the 3 clogged arteries and commented on how two of them had started to naturally by-pass themselves with thousands of blood vessels. Albeit not to the point of doing any major corrections, but it was most likely a factor for me not having a heart attack and being able to walk off the tennis court that evening.

He then had one of the students check my vein in my right arm; they were going to use a vein from my arm, leg and chest membrane to do the by-pass. After his quick examination, it was determined that my arm was good to participate in the procedure. But when I told him that I was right handed, they checked my left, which also passed the test.

Once we finished up with the doctor, we met with his assistant to book my surgery date. The end was finally coming after so many weeks of appointments, being off of work and waiting. Debbie, his assistant, pulled out the scheduling book. I could tell that there were a few appointments for the next couple of weeks and no openings for me. She confirmed that he only does two surgeries a day and the next opportunity for me to be the primary candidate was Monday, April the 23rd. Damn, that was three weeks away, which seemed like an eternity. She explained that if I didn't want to take any chances on having my date moved, the 23rd was the best. I was disappointed, but reluctantly agreed. Little did I know that accepting this date as the primary didn't hold any credence as my surgery date was moved two more times.

The final piece to my research was actually arranged by my manager. He was currently working on his MBA and one of his peers was a doctor in the cardiology ward of St. Mike's. He introduced me to this doctor. I arranged a meeting for us after my consult with the Chief of Cardiology. I had Debbie call him on his cell and decided to meet at the coffee shop on the main floor of the hospital.

He did a great job in showing Lori and I what to expect after my surgery. First, he took us to the 4th floor, the intensive care unit. I read a lot about this part of my recovery and it was nice to be able to visualize what I would be coming into. I was a little shocked when I looked over at a gentleman, who just came out of surgery. He had tubes and tape all over him or so it appeared. I looked at Lori's face quickly; she looked a little shocked too. I grabbed her hand and smiled in an effort to let her know I was going to get through this.

The doctor also introduced us to the head I.C.U. nurse and her comment was the same: "You look awfully young to be coming in for a bypass!" I just smiled and said, "I know I get that a lot." From there, the doctor took us up to the seventh floor recovery ward. It was nice to see the floor where I planned on taking my recovery to the next level. The head nurse there also commented on how young I was. Man, that piece was getting boring already. Once we completed our tour, Lori and I felt much more at ease with the whole procedure.

Two days later, on Wednesday, April the 4th, Lori and I went back down to St. Mike's for my Pre-Admission Facility meeting at 8:45am, also known as a P.A.F. A P.A.F. visit covers a nursing assessment, a pre- and post-operative overview of your surgery, a family history overview, a physical with a doctor and a blood test, x-ray and E.C.G. The whole procedure takes the better part of a day or up to five hours to complete.

We started off with a video screening on the expectations and experience of having open heart surgery. I looked around the boardroom table in the room that we were in and noticed that everyone was quite a bit older than me. And then, I noticed that there was actually one other gentleman, who appeared to be about my age. Thank goodness. Maybe no one will comment on how young I looked, which was like getting a loaf of bread that is brought out too often and stale!

I couldn't help but notice that he didn't seem too happy. Of course, no one was excited to be sitting through an open heart surgery screening, but we all seemed to be dealing with it in a positive manner. After the screening, I met up with this fellow and his wife while waiting for our chest x-ray. After a brief conversation, I found out that my impression of him was correct. He was really pissed at being diagnosed with heart disease. When I asked him how this all came about, his wife spoke up on his behalf, which can't be a good story.

Apparently, he was 47 years of age and didn't attend any of his regular check-ups. He was like your average man and afraid of going to doctors. In fact, he said that his last physical was five years ago and at the time, his doctor requested that he go in for a stress test. However, he took that requisition form and placed it on the sun visor of his car for four years. Now, he wondered how the heck he could have been diagnosed with heart disease when he had zero symptoms, no family history, no high blood pressure or high cholesterol - nothing! He was definitely the driver of the bitter bus on his way to pity city!

I looked him in the eye and said, "Buddy, do you realize just how lucky you are to be getting a second chance at life?" I mentioned how a lot of guys, or weekend warriors, don't get that second chance to go home to their wife and kids or get to be sitting where you are right now getting prepared to go under the knife in order to save your life. I concluded by telling him that, "You and me, my friend, have been truly blessed and need to seize this opportunity for what it is!" When I finished, his wife just smiled in agreement and then, the x-ray technician called me in for my procedure.

As I was getting my x-ray, I couldn't help but think how much of a pompous ass I was. Who was I to jump up on my soap box and tell him what I thought? I promised myself that I would not be that person before, during and after my surgery. I made a promise to myself that I would inspire and motivate people to avoid heart disease, but I wouldn't preach. I decided to apologize to him as soon as I got back to the waiting room.

When I opened the door and came out of the lab, he actually jumped up and met me half way across the room and shook my hand. He thanked me for my inspirational words and wished me the best of luck with my surgery. Wow, I guess I didn't preach after all and actually motivated him to a new place with his diagnosis. I couldn't help but think that this was what I wanted to do as a volunteer survivor speaker for the Heart and Stroke Foundation. The drive home had a whole different meaning as I daydreamed about being a spokesperson for the Foundation.

A couple of weeks later, on April 19th, the day before I was to confirm if my surgery was going to be in the morning or in the afternoon, they actually called me. I thought that they were moving me up at day or two for my surgery. Not! They were calling to tell me that my surgery had to be moved out - not a day or two, but 3 weeks! My heart sank; we had done everything that the doctors and their staff had suggested in order to get my caregiving lined up. Lori had booked vacation with work, Megan would be done with her exams and my sisters, Debbie and Cheryl, were on call should we need them.

I explained this to the surgeon's administrative assistant and told her that I had done everything that they suggested and that a 3 week delay was unacceptable - a two or three day delay I could deal with. If this delay was to take place, then quite frankly they were setting me up for a huge failure. They were altering my ability to have an outstanding recovery. She said that she understood and would speak to the triage coordinator and call back tomorrow. I went to bed that night with hope that my delay would be minimal. I asked my guardian angel to assist me and hoped my Dad was listening.

The next day, she called as promised; I crossed my fingers as she spoke. She told me that the three week delay was my only option. Then, I requested to have my surgery moved to another hospital with another surgeon. She said that I could make that request through my cardiologist. I explained to her that I didn't have a tight relationship with my cardiologist. I only met him due to my diagnosis and didn't have history with him as I did with my family doctor. It looked like May 11th was going to be my surgery date after all.

However, a couple of hours later, she called back to say that the doctor had made a request over at Sunnybrook to see if they could fit me in next week and would let me know in a day or two. When I didn't hear from St. Mike's that Monday or Tuesday, I called the doctor's office and spoke to his administrative assistant. She was shocked that I didn't heard anything yet. I asked if she could intervene and assist me with this request. She accepted and said that she would call me later that day. I hung up and looked at the clock; it was 11:30 am. We're not dealing with a lot of time here. I told Lori that I wasn't too confident on hearing back today.

I was wrong. The triage coordinator called just after 4pm to say that Sunnybrook hospital couldn't take me until the following week so it made sense that we just keep my appointment with St. Mike's. I shrugged and thought to myself, "At least they tried. I guess my surgery date will be May 11th now after all." But I was wrong again because the next thing she said was that my surgery was booked for this Friday, April the 27th at 8:30am. I was instructed to come to the 5th floor at 7:30am. I hung up the phone and thought, "Holy cow! The 27th is only two days away." I felt like I had just won the lottery, but I was also nervous. I decided to re-read all of the hospital literature that I was provided. The following day, I sent a note to the doctor and his staff to thank them for all that they did to get my surgery back on track. The lesson I learned here is that you need to push for what is right and don't allow the "system" to rule your life. Through my requests, they were somehow able to delay my surgery by 4 days, not 3 weeks. When I went to bed that night, I couldn't get over how nervous and anxious I was starting to get. You have to be careful about what you wish for, but at least my R and D (research and delays) were over for now.

With my buddy Scott who had his Dad Mel reach out to me

Lori, Marie, Scott and I enjoying ourselves as usual,
Scott was a great help to my surgery preparation

Ken & Leesa Armstrong who assisted Lori and I before my surgery in sharing Ken's journey and during when Leesa stayed with Lori at the hospital

GET YOUR BLOOD PRESSURE UNDER CONTROL

Blood pressure pamphlet

COPING WITH STRESS

Coping with stress pamphlet

Dealing with depression pamphlet

Recovery road booklet

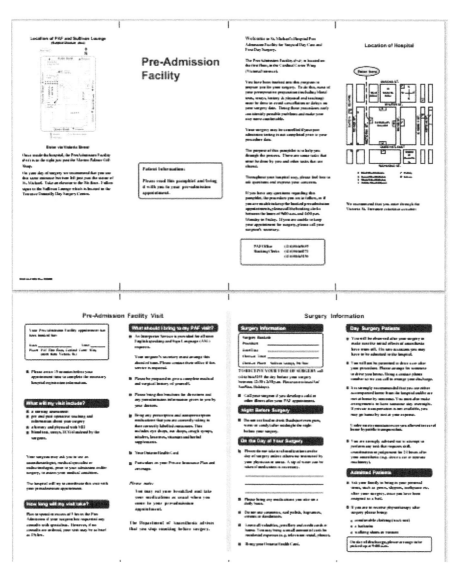

St. Michaels Hospital Pre-Admission Pamphlet

Salmon Cakes with Lemon Sauce

Salmon Cake Ingredients
1 can (7.5 oz/213 g) sockeye salmon, drained, flaked
½ cup (125 mL) cold mashed potatoes
½ cup (125 mL) dried whole grain bread crumbs
1 egg white, lightly beaten
¼ cup (50 mL) finely diced celery
1 green onion, finely chopped
1 Tbsp (15 mL) non-fat mayonnaise
2 tsp (10 mL) Dijon mustard
1 tsp (5 mL) grated lemon zest
¼ tsp (1 mL) pepper
¼ tsp (1 mL) cayenne pepper
1 Tbsp (15 mL) canola oil
Sauce Ingredients

½ cup (125 mL) non-fat yogurt
1 tsp (5 mL) lemon juice
1 tsp (5 mL) grated lemon zest

In a large bowl, combine salmon, mashed potatoes, bread crumbs, egg white, celery, green onion, mayonnaise, mustard, lemon zest, pepper and cayenne pepper. Form into 8 cakes. In a large non-stick skillet, heat canola oil over medium heat. Cook salmon cakes, turning over once, until golden and just cooked through, about 6–7 minutes. Meanwhile, in a small bowl combine yogurt, lemon juice and zest. Serve salmon cakes with sauce. Makes 4 servings.

Nutritional analysis - per serving (2 salmon cakes with 2 Tbsp/25 mL sauce)
Calories: 190
Protein: 16 g
Total Fat: 10 g
Saturated Fat: 1.5 g
Cholesterol: 35 mg
Carbohydrates: 12 g
Fibre: 1 g
Sodium: 430 mg

Recipes from the Quick and Healthy Cookbook developed by The Heart and Stroke Foundation and Manitoba Canola Growers Association

Chapter 7 – The Main Event

"One of the most sublime experiences
we can ever have is to wake up feeling
healthy after we have been sick."

- Harold Kushner
American Rabbi, born 1935.

The day before my surgery, I felt like I was walking around in a trance and in another world all together. After six weeks of waiting, the main event was right around the corner. The last thing I did, before going to bed that night, was shower and scrub my body with an antiseptic soap called Chlorhexidine to assist in preventing any surgical site infections. They instructed that you do your entire body, but pay special attention to your, chest, inner legs, groin and inner forearms, which I had to repeat in the morning. The smell of the soap really made me feel like I was already in the hospital; it had that "clinical" smell. I went to bed that night thinking about recovery road. I was definitely scared, but in the end, I guess I just wanted to get it over with.

The morning of my surgery, I was up early and showered with the antiseptic soap one more time. I looked at my body and wondered what my scars were going to look like, how my recovery was going to go, and if everything was going to be ok. I decided to reach out to my guardian angel one more time and asked my Dad to take care of me for my family and I. I just wanted to survive this so that I could be healthy once more and eventually walk my daughters down the aisle on their wedding days. The funny thing about those conversations is that they're a monologue, not a dialogue. You never really know if you have been heard, but in my heart, I truly felt that I was in good hands, both my Dad's and my cardiac surgeons.

On the drive down to the hospital, my eldest daughter, Megan, joined us as she wrote her final University exam that day - her school was literally walking distance from the hospital. I think it made her feel better to be joining us that morning; I know Julie and Kelly were a little apprehensive going to school that morning. Megan's exam wasn't until later that morning, so she actually got to help her mom get me settled in at the hospital. When I arrived, I was taken to a room where I was asked to put on my gown and to bag all of my personal belongings. I laid down on a gurney as I waited for them to come and usher me into the operating room. Usually I would mask my fear and concerns with my sense of humour, but I couldn't help but think about John Ritter, the actor who passed away a few years ago before my surgery. The story goes that he joked with his family before going into surgery that he didn't survive. With that in mind, I just laid there and stared at the walls waiting for my gurney driver to come and get me. When they arrived and told Lori and Megan that I was going off to the operating room, I just smiled awkwardly and said, "See you on the other side." I really couldn't say much; I was choking back tears and didn't want them to see my fear and anguish. I wanted them to think that I was strong and in control. The last thing I remember was the foot of the gurney hitting the operating doors. The room was extremely white and bright and there were a lot of people bustling around. I heard the anesthesiologist whisper in my ear and say, "Don't worry Mr. Campkin, everything is going to be………" I didn't hear another word; I was out like a light.

The best thing about open heart surgery is that you sleep through it and boy, did I sleep through it. For Lori, however, that wasn't the case as she waited for some word on my progress. Fortunately, after Megan left to write her exam, her brother John his wife Kerry and Ken Armstrong's wife, Leesa, joined her. Ken had just gone through his by-pass surgery a few weeks earlier, so Leesa provided great comfort to Lori. This gave her some much needed company as they sat in the waiting room waiting for my results. Here are Lori's comments on what that process was like for her.

There was never really a timeline given to Brian and me regarding the length of his surgery. We knew it wasn't an hour long procedure, but all we could do was hunker down for what would seem like an eternity. I was very grateful for all the support I had and half way thru the surgery, a family friend came to the hospital. Her husband, Ken, had just had by- pass surgery a few weeks prior to Brian and she came with lots of knowledge and support.

After about 3 hours, Brian's doctor came in the waiting room to talk to another person about their loved ones status. I remember being quite concerned that he wasn't with my husband. As it turns out, the surgeon isn't present for the whole surgery, there are different teams that work on the patient. When the 4 hour mark hit, the surgeon then came to us and said everything had gone well and that he was very pleased with Brian's stats. I wasn't too sure what that meant. Other than his clogged arteries, Brian was a very young, healthy man and that set the course for his very successful recovery.

Saying that I was scared is most certainly a huge understatement. When you are faced with such a life threatening circumstance like that, all you can do is face it all one day at a time. Lots of prayers, knowledge and support helped me to get through it all.

At the urging of the head nurse in the I.C.U. I went home just before dinner time to tend to my family and their needs. The nurse then provided me with a phone number directly to her workstation and said to call her in a few hours for an update. When I got home, I made dinner for the girls and me and then, after the dishes were done, I decided to call the head nurse. She picked up on the second ring and I introduced myself. She said, "Oh hello Mrs. Campkin your husband is doing great. In fact when he first woke up, the first thing he did was ask for a Peña Colada, do you have any idea why he would have done that?" I started to chuckle, "And said no he doesn't even like Peña Colada's, but I know one thing. If he was thinking about sitting at a swim up bar, then I have think he is well on his way to recovery." That conversation put my mind at ease as I knew that the worst was over and it was up to Brian to take on his recovery.

My first recollection post-surgery was waking up in the intensive care unit or I.C.U. as they called it, wanting my favourite take-out coffee. I must have been a pretty good salesman in my hallucinating state because I was able to convince the head nurse to oblige. After getting my small coffee, I recall throwing it up all over the place. To say that my nurse wasn't pleased would be a huge understatement. The last thing I remember before passing back out was her scolding me for the terrible mess I had made of myself.

The next morning, I woke up and was totally coherent. I did notice that the I.C.U. was very busy and noisy with a lot of bright lights. For the first time I was able to look at the damage that had been done to me. I had a bandage down the center of my chest, as well my left forearm and left calf. They were used to harvest the veins to do my actual by-pass. I was fairly comfortable, but extremely thirsty. The nurse said that this was normal due to the medications I received for my operation and because I had nothing to drink or eat well before my surgery. She gave me small doses of water to start to alleviate my thirst, but they were sensitive because I had thrown up my coffee earlier.

To control my pain, I was provided some pain killers through my I.V. and given some orally as well to keep me as comfortable as possible. I was actually quite surprised at how minimal the pain was for me, albeit I wasn't jumping out of bed or anything like that. In fact, to change positions in bed, I needed the nurse to assist me that first day. They wanted me to start moving right away and encouraged me to get up out of bed as soon as possible so that I could begin my recovery. This excited me because the ball was back in my court. The typical stay in the I.C.U. is one day and then, you're transferred to the recovery floor. In my case, however, it didn't happen because there wasn't a bed for me.

I had the worst sleep ever that night; the noise in the I.C.U. was unbearable. The nurses weren't concerned about the noise. Their patients were all out of it as if they hadn't fully come off the anaesthesia yet. When I woke up Sunday morning, I was tired and miserable. The head nurse for the morning shift came over and told me that there was a bed on the recovery floor was available, but there was no nurse available to take care of me. I thought that I was going to snap. I told her that if the surgery didn't kill me, then not getting to the recovery floor will. I explained to her how terrible my night was and she said, "Mr. Campkin, I am an A personality and I will promise you that it won't happen again. We will move you and your neighbour here, who is also stuck in this ward, to the other side of the floor for tonight's rest."

When she said that she was an A personality, she wasn't joking. She told me later that morning that it was time for me to become independent. When I asked her what that meant, she said, "You need to get up and move around. We are putting your I.V. on a pole with wheels so you can do just that." I was nervously excited about this. I was excited to begin my recovery, but nervous that one of the eighty-six staples holding me together may pop out at any time. I took my first few steps of freedom quite diligently, but very cautiously. It was painful to even try to get out of bed because usually Lori or one of the nurses would assist me. As I went through this process, I decided to just listen to my body as my family doctor had advised me so many weeks ago. If I got tired, then I would just go back to bed and lay down. By lunch time, I was moving around pretty well. I remember one of the on staff doctors, who was taking some Chinese exchange students through the ward, commenting on what a wonderful and amazing patient I was. He kept stating how he had never seen anyone move around the I.C.U. so shortly after surgery. His words made me feel great and gave me a sense of encouragement to try even harder.

The best I felt in the I.C.U. was that Sunday afternoon when Lori gave me my first sponge bath. I can't tell you how relieved I was to feel clean. Then, I spent the balance of the afternoon taking some short trips around the ward and got some rest. I even had a few visitors come and see me, which was awesome. Everyone kept saying how great I looked, but I sure didn't feel like it. I was in a bit of discomfort and longed for a proper shower to wash my hair. Just after dinner, our head nurse came over with her staff to move us to the other side of the ward. The last thing I remember before falling asleep was thinking that I would be on the recovery floor first thing tomorrow. As my nurse promised, it was the best sleep I had in a long, long time.

Monday morning arrived and I was excited to finally be on my way to the recovery ward. True to their word, I was wheeled away from the 4th floor I.C.U. and delivered to my new nurse on the 7th floor. I was starting to see the light at the end of the tunnel and was excited to finally be leaving the 4th floor. I don't want you to think that my care and attention in the I.C.U. was terrible. In fact, it was the exact opposite. I had a 1:1 patient to nurse care, provided back rubs, sponge baths and countless cups of ice chips to ward off the dryness and thirst I was constantly feeling. However, it was noisy and I had no access to the outside world - no T.V. or windows, nothing.

The 7th floor was great too. The nurses were busily bustling around with a constant sense of urgency. There seemed to be a steady stream of pages over the intercom with code blues or nurses to room, but it quieted down at night, which was a big relief for me.

When I was wheeled into my room and assisted into my bed, I met my assigned nurse. After a few pleasantries were exchanged, I told her that I wasn't going to use my call button and bother her to come and assist me in and out of bed; I wanted my freedom. She smiled and said, "Mr. Campkin, I will make you a deal. As I understand it, you were down in the I.C.U. all weekend so your recovery could be ahead of my normal first day patients. So with that in mind, if you can make 5 trips to the patient lounge and back again before I drop off your lunch tray, then we'll talk. Sound good?" I grinned and said, "Hell yes!"

With that, I spent the morning acclimatizing myself to the recovery floor and the patient lounge. And true to her word, my nurse came in around noon with my lunch tray. She placed it on the table in front of me and said, "Well Mr. Campkin, how did you do with your walks this morning?" I grinned broadly and said, "Well nurse, I took on your challenge and here is what I found out. Your magazines in the patient lounge are quite outdated. I already knew who shot J.R. in the T.V. program, *Dallas from the 80's,* and that old man in the blue terrycloth bath robe was hogging the convertor to the T.V. I'm also not really a *The Price is Right* fan. So after making 4 trips to the lounge, I wandered over to the other side of this ward and found a nice library where I sat and leafed through some books. How does that sound to you?" She grinned broadly and stated, "Well don't we have us a championship walker here? You, my friend, are free to come and go out of your bed without the call button." I smiled to myself quite proudly and did an imaginary fist pump. My first recovery goal was completed successfully.

In the early afternoon, I finally got the green light to have my first full shower, albeit I had to use a chair to sit in - I wasn't fit enough to endure standing for that length of time yet. I was excited to finally be able to take a bar of soap to my entire body and to wash my hair. I gathered my things and a nurse showed me to the shower facility. She was a very attractive, young lady. When she took me to the room, I was surprised at how large it was. She gave me a quick tour and then, ushered me to the oversized shower stall. She explained how everything worked and told me that there was a hand-held shower head to make it easier for me to rinse myself.

I thanked her for the tour and waited for her to leave before getting into my routine. She stood there for what seemed like a few minutes, which felt kind of awkward. Finally she said, "Mr. Campkin, I am here to assist you with your shower should you feel it necessary." I thought to myself, "If being diagnosed with heart disease didn't almost kill me, certainly being showered by this young lady so soon after my heart surgery surely would!"

Then, I remembered what Mel had told me a few weeks ago about having your "Jimmy Johnson" and body poked and prodded at when you're at the hospital. With that in mind, I smirked to myself and let her know because I was in the I.C.U. over the weekend, I was way ahead in my recovery and felt that I would be fine to shower myself.

She reluctantly agreed; I believe the normal protocol for new patients in the recovery ward is to have an assisted shower for the first time. She left and I locked the door behind her and began to have my shower. However, every minute or two, or so it seemed, she would knock on the door to ensure that I was ok. It was nice that she cared so much, but she kept disturbing my relaxing first shower. I finished up and put on some clean P.J.'s that Lori had brought and for the first time in a long time, I felt like a million dollars. The nurse then, ushered me back to my room. As I settled into my bed, I chuckled out loud to myself when I thought about Mel and the whole Jimmy Johnson thing again. Then, I dozed off for a well needed afternoon nap.

Later that day, I was able to see Lori and my three girls for the first time since my surgery. I was choking back tears as they all clamored into my room. I wanted to freeze the picture in my mind of them four smiling from ear to ear at the end of my bed. We had a great visit and chat. I even had some visitors from work come in, so we went down and spent most of the afternoon in the patient lounge to entertain my visitors. It was an awesome day, but it really wore me out. At 7pm, all was quiet; I put on the T.V. and before I knew it, I was fast asleep. I remember dreaming about walking out of the front doors of the hospital on my way home and thought that day could be tomorrow.

When I woke up on Tuesday, May the 1st, I had my sights firmly planted on my goal of going home. I was told that there were a few milestones for me in order to make this happen. One, I had to watch a going home video. Two, I had to have the wire in my chest removed, which was there as a precaution should they have had to put a pacemaker on me during my surgery. And three, I had to be able to have a bowel movement. Now, the first two seemed pretty easy, but the third one scared me a bit. I knew that they wanted to test my ability to put some strain on my chest.

I watched the going home video as planned and thought, "Yes, check number 1 off the list!" Later that afternoon, I attempted to test my chest pain threshold when a nurse banged on the door and yelled, "Mr. Campkin, are you in there? You need to take your pills." Just like that, my hardest goal suffered some stage fright. Damn, that one eluded me for the time being. Fortunately, later in the afternoon, I was successful at getting a missile in the chamber and at launching. "Yes, check the number 2 off the list!" I kept asking my nurse about having this temporary wire removed, but it didn't happen before the end of the day. My nurse told me that there was a standard procedural wait time of 4 hours after having the wire removed before I could go home. So I set my sights on Wednesday, May the 3rd as my departure date.

When I awoke the next morning, my nurse on staff stated that there was an urgency to get me out today because they needed the bed for another patient. I was excited by this and was truly hoping to leave on or before noon. I had the wire pulled around 9:30am. I have to admit that there was some considerable pain when they did it, but I just thought "No pain, No gain." All I needed now were my paperwork and prescriptions and then, I would be good to go. My nurse told me that they let Lori know and that she should be prepared to come and retrieve me around 12 today. Yes, my exit plan was all coming together now. I grabbed a shower and finally, got out my pyjama pants and into my blue jeans, which felt amazing

I went down to the patient lounge to work on my journal. I was keeping about my journey when I met a guy, who was 48 years of age. We both commented on how young we were to be here. We had a great conversation. He asked me a lot of questions about my experience, especially about the pain. Once we were done, I think he felt much more at ease. I was really pleased that I was able to do this for him. I then, went back to my room to say goodbye to my 84-year-old neighbour. He had been there when I arrived and now, I was going home before him. This made me realize that although getting heart disease is no fun, getting it at a younger age can work in your favour for sure.

My paperwork arrived and after a few comments and signatures, a wheel chair was brought to take me out. I looked at the chair and then at my nurse. Before I knew it, I blurted out, "I'm not going in that thing. No way! I promised myself that I would walk out of this hospital on my own free will." The nurse smiled and said, "Sorry Mr. Campkin. This is hospital policy. We cannot avoid this one." She saw the disappointment in my face as I sat myself into the chair.

She asked Lori where she had parked and when she replied that we were on the east side of the building, I could see the nurse smile. I thought that it was weird, but thought nothing of it. We headed out of the room as Lori carried my oversized travel bag and went down the elevator to the first floor. We got to the east side doors and I smiled broader than the Grand Canyon. Right before the doors, there were five steps and no ramp for the wheel chair. Now I know why the nurse had smiled. She was letting me achieve my goal by walking out on my own. I jumped out of the chair and took the five steps out to the brilliant and bright sunshine, which felt like heaven on my face. I turned, smiled and waved at her. I said goodbye to the hospital, hopefully forever.

Megan and I in 2007

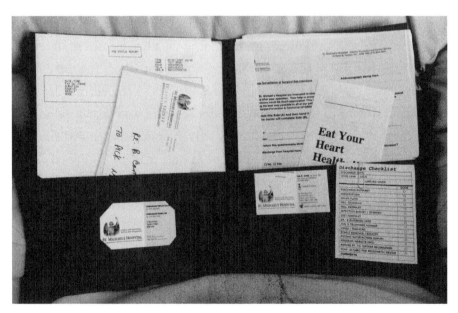

My discharge package from St. Mike's the day I left the hospital

St. Mike's Take It To Heart cardiac rehabillitation booklet I got when I left the hospital

The girls and I with my hospital gift

Turkey Tacos Three Ways

Ingredients
1 Tbsp (15 mL) canola oil
1 onion, diced
1 clove garlic, minced
1 tsp (5 mL) chili powder
1 tsp (5 mL) cumin
1 tsp (5 mL) paprika
¼ tsp (1 mL) pepper
1 lb (500 g) lean ground turkey
1 cup (250 mL) canned lentils, drained and rinsed
½ red pepper, diced
½ green pepper, diced
12 taco shells
1 cup (250 mL) chopped tomatoes
1 ½ cups (375 mL) chopped lettuce

¼ cup (50 mL) reduced-fat Monterey Jack cheese
¼ cup (50 mL) non fat sour cream, optional

Directions
In a large saucepan, warm canola oil over medium heat. Add onion and sauté until softened, about 4 minutes. Add garlic, chili powder, cumin, paprika, pepper and turkey and continue to cook for 8 – 10 minutes, until turkey is cooked through and there is no longer any pink colour remaining. Add rinsed lentils, red pepper and green pepper. Heat through, about 3 – 4 minutes. Place 2 tbsp (25 mL) of turkey mixture into taco shell. Top each taco with lettuce, tomatoes, and 1 tsp (5 mL) of cheese (1 tsp (5 mL) of sour cream optional). Makes 6 servings.

Tip: Leftover turkey mixture can be refrigerated and used in turkey taco wraps or turkey taco salad

Nutrition Analysis – per serving (2 tacos)
Calories: 360
Total fat: 10 g
Saturated fat: 2 g
Cholesterol: 40 mg
Sodium: 240 mg
Carbohydrates: 26 g
Fibre: 4 g
Protein: 26 g

Recipes from the Quick and Healthy Cookbook developed by The Heart and Stroke Foundation and Manitoba Canola Growers Association

Chapter 8 – Coming Home

"Our business in life is not to get ahead
of others, but to get ahead of ourselves
– to break our own records, to outstrip
our yesterday's by our today."

~ Stewart B. Johnson, Author

was very nervous about being in a vehicle for the first time after my surgery and I hoped that the seatbelt across my chest wasn't going to hurt. As it turned out, I could feel every little bump in the road. I was in some considerable discomfort sitting in the back seat of our truck on our way home. It was like I was riding in a taxi after open heart surgery and I couldn't risk sitting in the front seat with the air bag deploying. The thought of that just made me wince and it even opened my tear ducks a bit.

Lori did a great job manoeuvering the truck on the way home and we both decided that it would be good idea to drop off all of my prescriptions at the local drug store since there were a number of them to be filled. She decided to take a calmer route into the plaza and went through the back way. It seemed like a brilliant idea at the time, but she didn't know where the speed bumps were in the parking lot. After a few moments, it happened. BAM! We hit a speed bump at a pretty good clip. I'm not sure what scared Lori more, the sound that exploded from my mouth as the seat belt locked across my chest or the sound of my head hitting the interior roof of the truck. Once she came to a stop, she starting apologizing profusely; I just grinned and said not to worry. We dropped off the paperwork to be filled and headed home without further incident.

When I walked in through the front door, Jackson was all over me. I think I was more wet from all the kisses he gave than I was when I had my first sit down shower in the hospital. It was nice to know that even though we haven't had him for a long time, my new little, four-legged fitness trainer missed me. I planned on walking him as part of my initial recovery walks.

Before getting into the walking curriculum that day, I needed to do work on the fundraising for the charity walk team that I was the captain of. Going through all of my tests and eventual surgery put me way behind in this process. I sent out a blanket of emails to my network letting them know that I was alive, well and still planned on walking the 60KM walk the first weekend in September and if could they support me. It was the green light that everyone was looking for to reach out to me because I got a lot of replies and donations. Some just needed to know that I was up and around so that they could say a heartfelt hello.

Then, I started to go through the paperwork that I was given when I left the hospital. The last piece of paper I received was a walking curriculum to begin my recovery. It was based on achieving 28 levels over a period of time, which I felt that I could do. With my competitive spirit, I immediately set my site on doing the series of 28 walks in 28 days. My first walk consisted of doing a total of six five-minute walks in one day. By the end, I would be up doing one thirty-minute walk, which seemed quite daunting at this stage. But a journey begins with the first step and with that in mind, I had Lori tie up my running shoes, grabbed Jackson's leash and headed out for the first of our many walks.

I was able to make it five houses down and back again in five minutes during our first walk. I was really surprised at how easily tired and sore I got. On the second trip, I held a pillow across my chest to avoid any unwanted movement in my chest. I also went one crack in the sidewalk further on each trip. As the quote said in the beginning of this chapter, I was just trying to outstrip my yesterday by my efforts today.

That philosophy worked well for me and from there, I set goals to reach the next lamp post, then to the next street corner, and then eventually, to the next block. This helped me complete this twenty-eight level walking program in thirty days. I was a little disappointed that I missed a couple of days walking, but I just didn't have the energy to do it. I was listening to my body and doing what was right and heck, I was now walking in thirty minute intervals my first month home. I was starting to envision myself back on the tennis courts in January when my winter league starts up again. Although it seemed like a lifetime away, I wasn't even sure if playing tennis again would be possible for me at the moment.

I really enjoyed meeting the neighbours along the way during my walks; the spring weather was amazing and many were outside. What they say about good neighbours is true; we had some drop off meals for us. One actually came over and cut and trimmed my lawn without being asked. Wow, people are actually amazing. I also noticed how Jackson started becoming a neighbourhood celebrity. It seemed like everyone knew him by his name and called me, "Jackson's Dad!" It made me laugh and think that maybe, we should have named him Hollywood.

The following Tuesday, after my arrival home, I was off to my first post-surgery doctor's appointment with my family doctor. I found it hard to believe that after only five days at home, they were going to remove my eighty-six staples. I was cautiously optimistic about this. It was great to have them removed, which meant that my recovery was progressing as planned, but I couldn't help but think that it was going to hurt. Fortunately, Megan, my eldest daughter, had taken a shining to constantly clean my incisions and the wounds were clean as a whip going into this procedure. Only three of the eighty-six staples hurt when pulled out, but I was relieved when the nurse completed this exercise.

Then, my doctor switched my painkillers to Tylenol 3's, which was ok, but the previous pain killers had done their expected damage by blocking me up like a dam. My doctor was a little concerned about this and told Lori to get me some prune juice to keep things moving - being constipated wasn't good for my chest wound. I still had some powerful pain killers, but decided to switch entirely to Tylenol so that I could better manage my pain and constipation. It turned out to be a good plan and a couple days later, I was back in business and back to normal.

After a couple weeks home, it was Mother's Day weekend and we were pretty busy due to having company over on Friday and Saturday. I found myself excusing myself from our company that Saturday night and going to bed very early since the activity ended up being too much for me to endure. Sunday morning, after a great night's rest, I found myself wide awake at 5:45am. It was way too early to get up and to disturb the house. I knew that once my feet hit the floor, Jackson would start barking and start looking for a friend to play with. Thus, getting up wasn't an option for me.

I wrestled for ten to fifteen minutes to get myself propped up on a couple of pillows to to watch the sports news on TV on mute so that I didn't wake Lori on her Mother's Day. I just got settled in and comfortable when out of nowhere my first sneeze snuck up on me like a school kid playing hide and seek. Just like the seat belt incident on the way home from the hospital, I'm not sure what scared Lori the most - the actual sneeze or the noise that I made as I screamed out in pain as my chest bore the burden and pressure of my sneeze. It took me some time to recover from that experience and to be in a position of no pain, but through grimaced teeth, I told Lori to roll over, go back to sleep and that I was fine. It couldn't have been further from the truth, but I didn't want to spoil "her day!" I found that it took me until Thursday to fully recover from both the over excursion of visitors and that fateful sneeze.

The following weekend was a long May weekend and based on last weeks over zealous approach, Lori and I decided to stay home. We picked up some flowers and soil for our gardens and decided to putter around them for the weekend. As she began digging in the gardens, I decided to give it a whirl and cut and trim my front lawn, which was a big mistake. I still wasn't ready for this type of activity and my chest hurt like hell when I stopped. Lori decided that I wasn't going to be able to assist with the gardens, but ask that Jackson and I keep her company outside as she pruned and planted. I realized why I was going to be off of work for at least three months before my doctor would send me back; my recovery was definitely going to be a journey of ups and downs.

The one thing I found to be quite funny was everyone's expectation of how they would find me when they would come to visit. They thought that I would be wrapped up in blanket and huddled up in the corner of a couch or chair, but I wasn't. I was up and about and not lounging in my PJs. I was always dressed in jeans or shorts and a t-shirt. I wasn't afraid to have the scars on my leg or arm visible and in some cases, people asked to see my chest scar. They were my trophies from having survived open heart surgery; thus, I was more than happy to appease them.

I started to receive a number of cards, gift baskets and well-wishers and received a variety of flower arrangements, heart healthy cook books and fruit baskets. The one gift that really caught my attention, however, was from my client, who personally drove all the way across the city from Mississauga to my home in Whitby to give me an Odyssey two ball putter and spend time chatting with me. I really appreciated the fact that he never talked about work or business once. He kept the conversation casual and personal. He finally told me to open my gift because I probably wouldn't know what it was. It wasn't too hard to tell that it was putter; it wasn't wrapped in a box or anything so the shape gave it a way. As I opened it and took a few practice swings, I wondered when I would ever get back to my passion of tennis. I decided to put down "getting out to a golf and country club and playing a round" as another recovery goal for myself.

Later that day, when the phone rang, one of the folks from my other customer asked if I would be the guest speaker at their annual charity golf tournament in support of the Heart and Stroke Foundation. I jumped at the opportunity and said, "Yes."

"What I had just gotten myself into," I thought. "Oh well, at least I was going to visit a golf club sooner than I had imagined, even though I won't be playing in the tournament." I looked at the calendar and realized that I had less than three weeks to get my speech prepared. I immediately grabbed a notepad and began taking some notes.

That evening, I got my second golf surprise, when one of the participants on my charity walking team called to let me know that she was going to hold a charity golf tournament in two weeks to raise funds for our team and she wanted me to be the M.C. "Wow, I should set a goal to win a million dollars and see if it began showing up like all this golf stuff," I thought. Of course, I knew that it was a pipe dream, but I was just amazed at all of the good things taking place in my life.

A couple of weeks later, I arrived at the golf course early so that I could be taken out on a golf cart to see all of the participants and to thank them for coming. If I thought the ride home from the hospital was bumpy, it was nothing compared to the golf cart excursion. We hit a few doozy bumps, but I survived it nonetheless. Driving around the golf course really got my dream and goal of getting back to golf fired up. I didn't realize how much I missed it until it was waved right under my nose. I was pretty nervous about emceeing the dinner, but I thought it went well since I had only been home for a month now.

The following Thursday, I went to see my cardiologist for the first time since my surgery. He looked over my file and looked over at me and said, "Wow, it has only been five weeks since your surgery and you look great!" This really made me feel good; it meant that all my hard work, goal setting and exercising was paying off. He checked me over and everything seemed fine and my scars were healing nicely. He asked if I had any questions and I said, "Yes I have three."

First, I asked him if he had any concerns with me doing a 60km charity walk the first weekend in September. He said that he thought it was a lofty goal for sure, but he couldn't say yes or no yet. It really depends on how well I did at my cardiac rehabilitation program, which I set as one of my major goals which began at the beginning of August.

For my second question, I explained how I was speaking at a charity golf tournament in support of the Heart and Stroke Foundation. I asked him if he could say one thing to this corporate audience what it would be. He said that if I could convey one message on being healthy, it would be:

→ If you smoke, stop!

→ Go for a regular check-up.

→ If you have high blood pressure, cholesterol or diabetes, take your medication.

→ If you don't know if you have any of these, get tested and if you don't, you will triple your risk.

→ Exercise five times a week.

→ Eat right, use common sense and listen to your body.

It was excellent advice from a very credible source and I had the closing to my speech.

For my last question, I stated that I didn't really know how to express it, He said, "Just blurt it out Brian." I asked, "When would I be able to get back to a healthy relationship with my wife?" He complimented me for have the courage to ask this question because most of his patients were too shy or afraid to ask. He said that I would be quite happy with his answer because all I had to do was be able to walk up two flights of stairs without being winded.

When he looked at my face, he was quite surprised. I was disturbed by this and he couldn't understand why. I told him that I would never be able to do two flights of stairs at my house. He was puzzled now. He said to me, "Brian, you have just told me how well you did with your walking curriculum when you got back from the hospital and how well you are doing now.

Whatever are you worried about?" I told him again that it was impossible for me to do two flights of stairs at my house. Again, he asked why. That's when I told him, "Doctor, you don't understand. I live in a bungalow. I don't have two flights of stairs!" He laughed uncontrollably. I stood up and shook his hand and thanked him for his time. "Two flights of stairs was nothing for me to accomplish any time soon," I thought.

When I got back home, I looked at the stairs and smiled. "I will conquer you soon enough," I thought. I decided to go out in the backyard and continue writing and practicing my speech for the upcoming golf tournament, which was only a few days away. Jackson was out back with me when he ran up the back patio stairs. I was nervous that he would fall through the railing, so I took off after him. Before I knew it, I had climbed the stairs too. I smiled and thought, "One staircase down and one to go!"

Afterwards, I continued working on my speech and realized how nervous I was. It's not that I was afraid to speak in front of an audience - I had done a lot of that in my role as a sales representative. I was nervous about a few things. First, I wanted to impress the Heart and Stroke Foundation's representative; I still had a passion to be a survivor speaker for them. Secondly, I was going to know a lot of the attendee's in the audience and I was hesitant to tell such a personal story in front of work peers, colleagues and customers. And lastly, I had always been an emotional person before my surgery. I just wanted to try and hold it together when I was in front of a couple hundred people since I was even more emotional after my surgery.

Finally, the day arrived. Lori and I jumped into our truck for the 45 minute drive to the golf club. Lori had to drive since I was still unable to drive myself due to the soreness in my chest, but at least I had graduated to the front seat and no longer looked like a taxi passenger riding in the backseat. I had been managing this account for over five years, so the moment we arrived, I started running into people that I knew.

The first person I met when we entered the club house was my manager, Dave. Before he thought about it, he blurted out, "Holy shit! You look amazing!" I schmoozed with a lot of folks as they arrived for the reception. It was nice to see so many familiar and friendly faces. As we sat down for dinner, I was excited to learn that the Heart and Stroke Foundation's representative was sitting at our table. I told her about my desire to be a volunteer speaker for the foundation and we exchanged cards. That's when my account manager piped up to say, "Hey Brian, maybe she should wait to hear you speak tonight before she promises you anything eh!" We all chuckled, but I couldn't help but feel even more pressure.

After the dinner and the awards part of the event were over, the V.P. of Sales from my account introduced me to share my story and journey with heart disease. I barely got through introducing myself and talking about my wife of twenty-four years and my three daughters when I had to take a strategic sip of my water. It was my way of pausing to hold back the tears and emotions that were beginning to well up inside me. I told my audience that I would likely need a few of these pauses tonight, which got a good laugh and sent me on my way. Then, I decided to just speak from the heart and let the tears fall where they may. In the end, they gave me a standing ovation and the wife of the honouree of this tournament, who had passed away ten years earlier from a sudden heart attack, came forth and told me that it was the best keynote they had ever had.

Then, the V.P. called me back up to the lectern and presented me with an authentic Johnny Bower autographed Toronto Maple jersey and an autographed Toronto Maple Leaf print. Wow, what an awesome gift! I'm the biggest Leaf fan in the world. In fact, when I thanked them for the gift, I told the audience that I was such a big Maple Leaf fan that when they cut me open for my heart surgery, I actually bled Maple Leaf blue. The audience all laughed and mingled as the evening wrapped up.

My boss, Dave, came running over and squeezed me - a bit too hard by the way - said that I was his hero. Others came over and shook my hand

and thanked me or shared similar experiences they have had with heart disease. Finally, Marilyn, the Heart and Stroke Foundation representative came over, pulled out my card and said that the foundation would be in touch.

I enjoyed the ride home with Lori as we spoke about the evening's event. I kept asking her if I was as good as the audience thought I was and she kept saying, "Yes Bri. You were great." I fell asleep that night dreaming about speaking in front of more audiences as a survivor speaker for the Heart and Stroke Foundation realizing just how much of a positive impact my story could have. Now, I knew how much of a difference I could make.

We found ourselves on our way downtown to finally have my post-surgery visit with my cardiac surgeon. Once again, Megan joined us on the trip to the city since she had another class to attend. My surgeon was pretty shocked at how great I looked six weeks after my surgery. This was really becoming a common theme for me and I truly believed that the outcome was due to my amazing attitude going into and coming out of my surgery. After my visit, we went up to the seventh floor recovery ward to do a quick walk around and say hello. I noticed just how close the patients lounge was to my room and how daunting of a goal it felt a short time ago. It made me realize just how far along I came in my recovery and what a difference it was to receive awesome care from Lori and my three girls, which was a key part to my awesome recovery. As we left the hospital, Megan took a picture of me in front of the St. Mike's sign with my favourite take out coffee… the same one I threw up in the I.C.U. a few weeks ago.

Walking with my buddy Jackson!

First weekend home after surgery with Lori and Jackson

Lori's Mother's Day 2007 and the day of my first sneeze

At my post surgery surgeon visit with my favourite cup of coffee

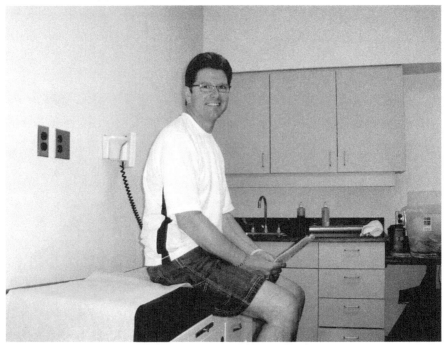

At my post surgery surgeon visit 6 weeks post surgery

Walking Program (Chart) *6-7 houses*

When you have completed this walking program you may be able to participate in a Cardiac Rehabilitation program offered at an institution close to home. Discuss this with your Cardiologist at your one month follow-up appointment.

Issaland

Levels	Min Walked	Frequency	
1	5	6	+++++ ꞁ
2	6	5	+++++
3	7	4	ꞁ ꞁ ꞁ ꞁ
4	8	4	ꞁꞁꞁꞁ
5	9	3	ꞁꞁꞁ
6	10	3	ꞁꞁꞁ
7	11	3	ꞁꞁꞁ
8	12	3	ꞁꞁꞁ
9	13	2	ꞁꞁ
10	14	2	ꞁꞁ
11	15	2	ꞁꞁ
12	16	2	ꞁꞁ
13	17	2	ꞁꞁ
14	18	2	ꞁꞁ
15	19	2	ꞁꞁ
16	20	2	ꞁꞁ
17	21	2	ꞁꞁ
18	22	2	ꞁꞁ
19	23	1	ꞁ
20	24	1	ꞁ
21	25	1	ꞁ
22	26	1	ꞁ
23	27	1	ꞁ
24	28	1	ꞁ
25	29	1	ꞁ
26	30	1	ꞁ
27	30	1	ꞁ
28	30	1	ꞁ

Take It to Heart | Cardiac Rehabilitation after Heart Surgery

My actual walking program chart that I used to track my 28 recovery walks

Showing off my scar with Megan my at home nurse maid

Lori's front garden Spring of 2007

Lori's back garden Spring of 2007, Jackson and I watched as I did not have the strength to assist her yet

My nehphew Dayne helps me cut the grass for the first time post surgery!

My friend Jennifer and her son Nicholas who brought me a lovely fruit basket when I got home from the hospital

One of the many gift baskets I received after my surgery

The welcome sign for our charity Golf Tourney that I was the emcee

Vic Oliver tournament with our MC Mark Ciprietti, Lori and I with my generous gifts

Chicken and Sweet Potato

Chicken and Sweet Potato Quessadilla Ingredients
2 tsp (10 mL) canola oil, divided
2 boneless, skinless chicken breasts, diced
1 tsp (5 mL) chili powder, divided
1 tsp (5 mL) dried oregano, divided
1 shallot, minced
2 cloves garlic, minced

1 small sweet potato, peeled and shredded
¼ cup (50 mL) sodium reduced chicken broth
½ avocado, mashed (optional)
6 small (7 inch /17.5 cm/) wholegrain tortillas
½ cup (125 mL) shredded lower fat cheddar cheese

Directions
In a large nonstick skillet, heat 1 tsp (5 mL) of canola oil over medium high heat. Add chicken breasts with 1/2 tsp (2 mL) each of the chili powder and oregano. Cook for 3 minutes or until starting to brown; remove to plate. Add remaining canola oil to skillet and cook shallot, garlic and sweet potato with remaining chili powder, oregano and broth for about 5 minutes and liquid is absorbed. Return chicken to skillet and cook, stirring until chicken is no longer pink inside. Remove from heat. Spread avocado among half of each side of all the tortillas, if using. Divide chicken mixture over top and sprinkle with cheese. Fold over tortilla to cover. In clean nonstick skillet toast que-

sadillas over medium heat for about 4 minutes turning once or until golden brown and crisp on both sides. Serve with Tomatillo Cucumber Lime Salsa.
Makes 6 servings.*

Tomatillo Cucumber Lime Salsa Ingredients
4 small tomatillos, husked and finely diced
1 cup (250 mL) finely diced English cucumber
1 clove garlic, minced
1 small jalapeno pepper, seeds removed and finely diced
2 Tbsp (25 mL) chopped fresh cilantro
2 green onions, finely chopped
1 lime, zest and juice
1 Tbsp (15 mL) canola oil
1 tsp (5 mL) granulated sugar

Directions
In a medium bowl, combine tomatillos, cucumber, garlic, jalapeno pepper, cilantro, green onions, lime zest and juice, canola oil and sugar. Marinate for 1 or 2 hours in the refrigerator. Transfer to serving dish. Fresh salsa will keep in the refrigerator for up to 3 days. Makes 8 servings.

Nutritional Analysis – per serving (1 tortilla with 1/6 filling & ¼ cup(50 mL) salsa)
Calories: 265
Protein: 15 g
Total Fat: 10 g
Saturated Fat: 1.5 g
Cholesterol: 25 mg
Carbohydrates: 28 g
Fibre: 3 g
Sodium: 330 mg

Chapter 9 – The Caregiver's Role

"For better and for worse, in sickness
and in health, until death do us part."

~ The Wedding Vow

When we get married, we find ourselves reciting the wedding vow. There's that infamous line that states, "In sickness and in health." I think that most of us utter these words to get to the end of our wedding ceremony, but we truly don't believe that we will need to act on this in our life time. But what do we do when it does, as it did for me when I was diagnosed with heart disease? In 2007, the year of my diagnosis, Lori and I were celebrating our 24th wedding anniversary and I can honestly tell you that we never spoke about how we would handle taking care of each other should the other get sick. But then, it happens and one of us is thrust into the caregiver role as our partner battles for their life.

That's what happened to Lori on the day of my diagnosis; she went from being a wife and a mother to also becoming a caregiver. Being a full-time caregiver is definitely an unfamiliar role and I know that Lori never imagined having to take on such a role. She immediately became the person who was tending to my every needs, both pre- and post-surgery.

She attended every one of my doctor's visit with me since we felt that it would be good for both of us to listen to what was going on with me just in case one of us missed something. We always discussed my visits in advance and what we wanted to get out of those sessions with the doctor. Then, on the way home, we would review what we learned to ensure neither of us missed anything.

We found this to be very good practice and one that I would recommend to anyone who is going through a similar experience. There is a lot going on for both the caregiver and the patient at this time. You are wrapped in a blanket of fear and emotion and we found that the more we learned about what we were going through, the more this blanket unravelled for us.

As I mentioned earlier, I wrote a blog for the Heart and Stroke Foundation for their website after my surgery. One of the columns was titled, "Taking care of my husband – the caregiver role," Which was written by Lori from the caregiver's point. I thought that I would take a moment to share it with you so that you can understand the impact of the role.

Taking care of my husband – The Caregivers role

When my husband came home one day from playing tennis complaining of shortness of breath, I urged him to have his doctor check him out. Even when his physician said he didn't think anything was wrong, I kept at Brian to dig deeper. I'm glad he did. But getting to the bottom of the problem took five weeks. When the nurse said, "Well do you want to tell her, or do you want me to?" Little did I know that those few words could be so life altering?

Our journey started at the hospital for a more in-depth stress test. When they asked us to stay put while the cardiologist had a look at the test results, I knew something was up. When the doctor finally finished reviewing the results, we were informed that there was some kind of blockage in the arteries of the heart and as soon as possible a test called an angiogram was to be done. That is when all the "fun" really began. "Brian needs bypass surgery" was all I heard when the tears started flowing. How could Brian, 46, always active and healthy need such a serious operation?

Our first job, after the shock of bypass surgery was given to us, was to go home and tell our 3 daughters that their Dad needed open heart surgery. Although I had not even had time to digest the totally unexpected news myself,

I had to be both reassuring to the girls that Dad was going to be OK and to Brian that he would not only recover from the surgery, but would probably feel better than he had in a long time. I think this reassurance for everyone else helped to totally convince me.

This is when my role as a caregiver began. I was fine in dealing with my children's runny noses and upset stomachs, but I had no idea what lay ahead for me dealing with my husband as a patient. I had almost zero experience with heart disease. Although Brian's Dad had a massive heart attack and died at 61, I didn't learn a lot about heart disease, as I was fairly young at the time. I knew of people who had bypass surgery, but I did not have any first-hand experience to rely on. I became like a sponge absorbing everything the doctors and nurses told me about all the things to expect. A great resource that I used to ramp up on my knowledge was the Heart and Stroke Foundation website. I accepted and read every pamphlet that was given to us at the hospital and doctor's office, many of which came from the Foundation. I also talked to a lot of people who had already undergone this operation.

As a caregiver, I felt one of my biggest responsibilities was giving Brian reassurance that all the things he was going through were normal. Thankfully, Brian was in a good position because of his age and excellent health. Because of this, I really did not have any fear that my husband was not going to be okay. Every doctor we spoke to was very reassuring that based on Brian's age and health, he should be just fine.

However, I think the hardest time was bringing Brian home from the hospital. Now it was in my hands, no doctors or nurses helping him, or making decisions on what was the best things for him. The first few days home were the toughest as Brian had very limited mobility, especially getting in and out of bed and going up and down the stairs. I also ensured that Brian started a schedule of taking his medication as he was not prone to taking more than an Advil before his surgery. It was imperative that he made this process apart of his routine going forward, like brushing his teeth.

It didn't take me more than a few days to have to begin telling Brian to slow down a bit. He totally took on his recovery walking curriculum and completed his 28 walks in 30 days. I was proud of him, but also a bit scared.

I knew that my health was important and that the stress that we were under was going to have some kind of impact on me. My girlfriends support, visits and long chats on the phone were a life saver for me. I would grab my music and go for long walks that always helped work off some stress. I have always enjoyed a long, hot bubble bath, but now it was like my own prescription and essential in helping me to relax.

I also found time to take care of our new puppy, Jackson, and have to admit that doting over him was a bit of a release for me. As we all know, if you want loyalty in your life, get a puppy. Taking Jackson on some short walks was also a great form of release for me as I tended to him and let my cares float away.

I was not only the caregiver, but I was also the one who received a lot of support. Our family and friends made sure that our freezer was full with dinners and I had lots of people with me at the hospital when Brian had his surgery. But most of all, I knew everyone's love, prayers and best wishes were with us through it all. Overall, Brian was a very good patient and the 4 ½ months that he was home and not working was a good indication that we will be able to retire together quite nicely.

As you can see from Lori's article, she was a rock when it came to her role as the caregiver. Sometimes life deals us a hand and we just have to accept it and play it, which was exactly what Lori did with me. She was my champion, my motivator and my day-to-day balance in dealing with this life changing event. I'm sure it was'nt easy for her, but she laid out a great game plan for herself and followed it through flawlessly. As they say, "Success isn't in the concept; it's in the execution." She balanced her role as a caregiver and didn't lose sight of the fact that she also had to take care of herself, which she did with her walks, bubble baths and time with her girlfriends. I don't know what I would have done without Lori's day-to-day support and encouragement, but I definitely know that having her as my caregiver was a major reason for my phenomenal recovery and experience.

Lori and I in 1978

Lori and I on our wedding day, June 18th 1983

Lori taking a well deserved soak in our hot tub

Lori talking Jackson for a walk along the pier at the Whitby shoreline

Lori with her bank friends as I call them, Hilary, Terri and Marie

Lori with her brother John and Joe along with Karen and her Mom

Lori with her very good friend Marie along with Bernie and Jackson

Lori with Julie, her sister Karen, her Mom Marion and Kelly

Lori with our good frienid LeeAnne

Lori with our neice Brooke

One of Lori's quiet moments, well sharing quality time with
Julie, Megan and Kelly. My four caregivers

I could not have recovered as well as I did without my awesome caregiver Lori

Oatmeal Blueberry Walnut Muffins

Ingredients
1/4 cup (50mL) soft non-hydrogenated margarine
1/2 cup (125 mL) packed brown sugar
1 omega-3 enriched egg or regular egg
2 egg whites
1 cup (250mL) oat bran
1 cup (250mL) large flake oatmeal
1/2 cup (125mL) 1% milk
1 tsp (5mL) vanilla extract
3/4 cup (175mL) whole wheat flour
2 Tbsp (25mL) ground walnuts
2 tsp (10mL) baking powder
1/2 tsp (2mL) baking soda
1 cup (250mL) fresh or frozen blueberries
Oatmeal crumble
1/4 cup (50mL) large flake oatmeal
2 Tbsp (25mL) chopped toasted walnuts

2 Tbsp (25mL) whole-wheat flour
2 Tbsp (25mL) soft non-hydrogenated margarine

Directions
In large bowl, stir together margarine and brown sugar until combined. Add egg, and egg whites, one at a time and stir until smooth. Add oat bran and oatmeal. Pour in milk and stir until moistened. Stir in vanilla.
In another bowl, whisk together flour, ground walnuts, baking powder and soda. Add gradually to margarine mixture and stir until almost all combined. Add blueberries and fold until well distributed.
Scoop out muffin batter into 12 muffin cups; set aside.

Oatmeal Crumble: In small bowl, stir together oatmeal, walnuts and flour. Using small spoon, mix margarine into the oatmeal mixture until combined. Gently press some of the crumble mixture on top of each muffin. Bake in 400°F (200°C) oven for about 20 minutes or until cake tester inserted comes out clean. Makes 12 muffins.

Tip: Wrap cooled muffins individually in plastic wrap and freeze for up to 2 weeks.

Nutritional Analysis per serving (1 muffin)
Calories: 192
Protein: 6 g
Total fat: 7 g
Saturated fat: 1 g
Dietary cholesterol: 16 mg
Carbohydrate: 30 g
Dietary fibre: 3 g
Sugars: 11 g
Sodium: 179 mg
Potassium: 184 mg

Recipe developed by Emily Richards, P.H. Ec. The Heart and Stroke Foundation.

Chapter 10 – Cardiac Rehabilitation

"Movement is a medicine for creating change in a person's physical, emo-tional, and mental states."

~ Carol Welch, Nutritional Consultant

Now that I had my initial walking curriculum behind me, it was time to engage in my cardiac rehab program. Before I could get the green light to begin the program, I actually had to have a stress test to prove that I was physically ready to take on this next challenge. I did the test at my doctor's office as I had a few months ago before I began this whole journey. There was a doctor and technician present this time, which I fully understood. I was actually happy that the two of them were going to see me beat the heck out of that treadmill this time, which is exactly what I did. I was going to keep on trucking until somebody yelled stop. I kind of felt like Forrest Gump, where he just gets up on the porch one day and runs and runs. He had no real mission in mind in his running; mine however had specific intent. Finally, the technician yelled that we were good and shut the treadmill off. I had reached another milestone by finally beating the treaded treadmill.

When they issued me the paperwork, I found out that my rehab was being held on the 11th floor of the hospital where I was first diagnosed. I have to admit that it felt really weird to be going back, but this time, there were no treadmills or tests that were going to get the best of me - no, not this time. I was excited to be taking this next step in my recovery and was looking forward to what this program was going to provide me. Before starting the physicality of my rehab, I had to attend some educational classes. At the end of June, I made my first trip to my class on heart facts. The following two weeks were about healthy eating and knowing your meds. We also had a physiatrist guest speaker, who spoke about dealing with depression.

After that class, I couldn't help but reflect on my own journey at this time and how depression had not been one of the post-surgery items that I had to deal with. The obvious concern after open heart surgery is our physical health, but it was interesting to hear our speaker talk about the emotional aspects of dealing with heart surgery. Depression is not like a broken bone; it doesn't show up on an x-ray. It's detected through behavioural and attitude changes. He mentioned one statistic that I found to be alarming: 33% of people diagnosed with heart disease end up developing some sort of depression. As I looked back, I truly believed that it was my amazing positive attitude and that I was afforded a second chance in this world that I was able to avoid becoming a part of this statistic.

On August 2nd, I attended my first real cardiac rehab session. The first thing I noticed was that the age group was very dynamic from people in their mid-forties to those who appeared to be in their early sixties. They split the classes into age groups and the older folks attended a different session that was at a slower pace. I was introduced to my therapist, Rajeanne, and after we exchanged some pleasantries, she asked me what I wanted to get out of my rehab experience. I shared my three major goals with her: doing the 60km charity walk, getting back to competitive tennis and walking my three daughters down the aisle on their wedding days.

She worked them back with me in the reverse order and asked how old my daughters were. When I told her that they were 19, 16 and 13, she said that we can probably push that goal out for now since they weren't getting married any time soon. I chuckled and agreed with her. Then, she asked me when my tennis league would be starting. I told her January and she put that one aside also, which I agreed with again. When she asked when the charity walk was and I told her that it was in six weeks, she said, "Bingo! We have us a beauty goal to reach for."

She took me over to a treadmill and said that we had to do one more stress test before getting started. We went through the paces and again, I outlasted the treadmill and got my green light to start my rehab. She took me on a tour of the facility and explained how the program would work. Essentially, we would arrive each week, have our blood pressure taken, grab out check list, string of beads, do our light weight routine, and then do our walking curriculum. The strings of beads were used to count your laps to monitor our progress so that they would know when to elevate our game, so to speak. With that, she told me about my routine for the night and I set off to do my walk. Before I left, I was given my walking routine for my at-home portion of the program.

I enjoyed doing the at-home walks since I could do them outside and set my own routes. I purposely set mine up to have a mix of level streets and a number of hills so that I could escalate my recovery. If I was going to do the 60K charity walk in six weeks, then I was going to have to make sure that I was absolutely ready to go. To monitor my progress, I used a heart monitor/watch that my niece, Katie, had given to me. It not only helped me watch my heart rate, but it also allowed me to monitor my time and track my progress while completing my walks.

Every week I went to rehab, I had a passion and goal to beat my previous week even if it were only ½ a lap or a few steps more than the previous week. Rajeanne kept commenting how phenomenal I was doing and that she truly saw me being able to join my team on the big walk, as we had come to call it. I also set a goal to increase the weights that I was using; I felt that just getting my cardio up wasn't enough and I had to improve my physical strength too. I found that by setting these small goals, it made the bigger goal seem much more achievable. As I reviewed my rehab tracker each week, it was apparent that I was successfully achieving these goals.

At the end of the month, I received a call from my charity walk coach out of the blue. The charity foundation lined all the captains of the walking teams with a coach, who was a member from their organization, should you have any questions or needs. This call surprised me because I didn't reach out to them at all. My coach went on to say that the CEO of the Foundation saw my posting on my donation page where I stated that I was leveraging this terrific walk to recover from open heart surgery and that he was totally touched and inspired by this. With that in mind, asked if I would speak at their closing ceremonies. "Absolutely, that would be an honour," I said. I had a picture flash in my mind of the ceremony I attended last year and did a quick estimation. There were about 5,000 people in that audience. When I asked her to confirm the number, she agreed that I was probably pretty close to the right answer. After I hung up, I thought, "Holy smokes! What have I just agreed to now?"

This put a whole renewed focus for me. There was no way I couldn't do the walk now that I agreed to speak at the closing ceremony in front of that many people. When I went to rehab the following week, I told Rajeanne and she said that it was amazing and I had her support in order to make this happen. With her on my side, I continued to do my walks every day - rain or shine - and quickly progressed through my curriculum. I was also doing training walks with my team on the side and part way through my rehab, we did a 12km walk through Rotary Park along the shores of Lake Ontario in Ajax. I really felt like I was going to reach that goal.

Finally, September the 8th, the day of the walk arrived. Our team of fourteen - family, friends and colleagues - were ready to take the streets of Toronto. I also had some family members participating as volunteers. It was nice to know that my whole family would be at the finish line the following day to see me cross the finish line.

To say that I was nervous would be a huge understatement. Walking the track at rehab and the streets of Whitby was fine, but now I was going to walk 60kms over the course of two days. When you set a goal of this magnitude, you don't really focus on the end. It's really about the journey and the little milestones. But here I was, standing with 5,000 other participants listening to the opening ceremonies from the Princess Margaret Hospital dignitaries, doctors and a handful of survivor speakers. They had a group of 5 to 6 survivors join hands in a circle and part the crowd down the middle as they made their way to the stage. I couldn't help but think about my Dad and my buddy, Mike, who were taken from us too early. I had a renewed vigor to complete this walk and with that, we all cried, cheered and commenced on our journey as we walked out of the Princes Gates at Exhibition stadium.

Shortly into our walk, we came into a park and when we made our way to the other side, there was a massive hill. My brother-in-law, John, who had decided to walk with me for safety reasons, looked at me and said, "So C, (his nickname for me) do you have this one in your bag?" I just smiled, winked and said, "Bring it!" When we got to the base of the hill, I was actually walking beside a gentleman, who had some form of disability; he was doing the walk in his wheelchair. I leaned over to him and asked if he wanted a hand. He looked at me, smiled and said, "No. I need to prove something here!" I smiled back and told him that I fully understood and decided to walk that hill beside him in his wheelchair so that we could conquer this goal together. When we got to the top, we high fived each other and went on our way; I had a huge adrenalin rush pushing me forward.

The rest of the day went fine as we meandered through the streets. So many people lined the streets with signs, cheering us on with every step that we took. Some even put out drinks, snacks and sprayed us with a water hose to cool us off. It was just an amazing day. We finished walking at about 4:30pm and completed close to 32kms as we entered the gates to Downsview Park, which was designated as the ½ way point. There were tents set up for those staying the night and a huge reception area for dinner and entertainment that night.

We didn't partake in the festivities; my team and I were headed back to my place in Whitby for dinner and a much needed hot tub. My massage therapist, Lesley, also came out to donate her time and provide everyone with a 20-minute massage to rejuvenate our sore and aching muscles. We all munched on some pizza, had a libation or two and then, hunkered down early that night. We had to be up at 6:00am so that we could have our shuttle drivers - my sister, Debbie and Cheryl, along with our friends Hilary and Joanie (Mike's wife), get us back to the park for breakfast and to start walking by 8am.

On Saturday, the first day of the walk, the weather was amazing. On Sunday, however, we woke up to rain. Not an ideal way to walk the final 28KMs, but we weren't going to let that disappoint us. We headed back to the park at approximately 8am and headed out to finish our walk. By lunchtime, the rain had subsided. Around three o'clock that afternoon, my largest recovery goal to date was in sight; I could see the gates into the exhibition. As we entered the gates, the sidelines were jammed with people cheering and clapping us into the finish line. As we turned the corner at the Better Living Centre building, I could see the finish line and my family and friends all lined up to watch me cross.

Then, I had a flood of thoughts going through my head. I thought of my Mom, who I created this walking team for in 2004, when she lost her battle with cancer. I thought of my Dad, who passed away 16 years earlier, and of course, my buddy, Mike, who had only left us a few short months ago. It was an emotional final few steps as I hit the finish line, but I was elated to have set and achieved such a huge goal in such a short time after my open heart surgery.

We all went into a holding area where walkers were provided drinks, snacks and an area to rest and put their feet up. Shortly afterwards, I was told that it was time for me to make my way to the stage. I told security that I needed my team with me. They told me that I was the only one able to come to the holding area behind the stage. I then asked, actually pleaded, if my team could get to the front of the line of walkers waiting to enter the area for the closing ceremonies. When I told him why I was chosen to speak at the closing ceremonies, he lifted the red tape. My team was able to get to the front of the line.

I immediately began pacing nervously when I got to the area behind the stage. How could this person, who almost failed Grade 5 because he would not do the public speaking assignment, get in a position to speak in front of 5,000 people? Then, the CEO of the Princess Margaret Hospital, Paul Alofs, came in. We chatted for a few minutes, which seemed to calm me down quite a bit. Finally, the time had come. I heard my name announced and made my way up to the lectern to deliver my speech. Out of the corner of my eye, I saw my entire team, family and friends standing in front of the stage. I tried not to look at them because I knew that if I did, I would have cried for sure. After my speech, all 5,000 people clapped and cheered as they heard me share my reasons for doing this terrific walk in honour of my Mom and to overcome my open heart surgery. As I left the stage, I was beaming as I thought to myself, "Alright! Bring on the tennis league in January. This guy is ready for his next big goal!"

With my rehab therapist and coach, Rajeanne

My cardiac rehabillitation workbook and information I received on day 1 of my rehab program

 Rouge Valley
HEALTH SYSTEM

Cardiac Care
Program

DO YOU KNOW
YOUR TARGETS?

Name: _____

Date: _____

To optimize "heart health", you need to know your own risk factors for heart disease. The table below will help you determine which healthy goals you have already met and which ones you still need to modify. Rouge Valley Health System is committed to working with you to reach these "healthy goals" when you reach home. These targets should be assessed by your Healthcare Professional and your Cardiac Rehabilitation Exercise Therapist.

	Your Current Status		HEALTHY GOAL			Your Current Status		HEALTHY GOAL
	Date	Value				Date	Value	
Total Cholesterol			<4.5 mmol/litre		Blood Pressure			<120/80 mmHg
LDL			<2.5 mmol/litre		Fasting Blood Sugar			< 7.0 mmol/litre
HDL			>1.0 mmol/litre		Waist			Male < 90 cm (36") Female < 88 cm (35")
TRIG			<1.7 mmol/litre		Smoking			Smoke free lifestyle
Exercise			30-60 minutes 5 times/week		Stress			Control of stress, anger and depression

Take this form to your Family Doctor to discuss your own risk factors and heart health.

M:\Cardiac Rehab\Cardiac Rehab Program Files\FORMS\Patient Treatment Forms\Healthy targets.doc
Last Updated September 2005 (LS)

One of the many forms that help guide me through my rehabillitation

The beads I used to count my walking laps at my cardiac rehab
and the gold heart lapel pin I was presented with when I graduated

Megan, Lori and I, day 1 of the 60K charity walk about 13km's of the way through our day

Simply the Breast walking team outside Princess Margaret Hospital
just a few KM's from the finish line

Crossing the finish line after walking 60 kilometres, four and half months after my surgery

Delivering my keynote in front of 5,000 people at the closing ceremonies of the
Weekend to End Breast Cancer 60K walk

Quinoa Raspberry Muffins

Ingredients
1/2 cup (125mL) quinoa
1/2 cup (125mL) orange juice
3/4 cup (175mL) 1% milk
1 ½ cups (375mL) all pur-
pose flour with added bran
(available at grocery stores)
1 1/2 tsp (7mL) baking
powder
1/2 tsp (2mL) baking soda
1/4 tsp (1mL) ground cinnamon
1/3 cup (75mL) packed brown sugar
1/4 cup (50mL) soft non hydrogenated margarine, melted
1 egg
1/2 tsp (2mL) vanilla
1 cup (250mL) frozen raspberries

Directions
Place quinoa in fine mesh sieve and rinse well. In small saucepan, combine quinoa with orange juice and 1/2 cup(125 mL)
of the milk. Bring to boil over medium high heat. Reduce heat
to low; cover and cook for 15 minutes. Remove from heat and
let stand for 5 minutes or until liquid is absorbed. In another
bowl, whisk together flour, baking powder, soda and cinnamon.
Stir sugar, melted margarine, remaining milk, egg and vanilla
into quinoa mixture and pour over flour mixture. Stir until

moistened. Stir in raspberries. Divide batter among 10 lightly greased or paper lined muffin cups.

Bake in 400 F(200 C) oven for about 18 minutes or until cake tester inserted in centre comes out clean.

Nutrition Analysis per serving
Calories: 194
Protein: 5 g
Fat: 5 g
Saturated Fat: 1 g
Cholesterol: 20 mg
Carbohydrate: 32 g
Fibre: 3 g
Sugar: 11 g
Sodium: 147 mg
Potassium: 175 mg

Recipe developed by Emily Richards, P.H. Ec. ©Heart and Stroke Foundation 2011

Chapter 11 – Recovery Road

"For everyone, well-being is a journey.
... The secret is committing to that
journey and taking those first steps
with hope and belief in you."

- Deepak Chopra
American Author, born 1947

was both physically and mentally exhausted after completing the walk
and doing my speech, but before I knew it, I was back at my rehab
class. Rajeanne congratulated me on achieving my goal and immediately asked me what my next goal would be for the fall. I told her that my
next big goal was to get back to tennis in January. As a good rehab coach,
she said, "Come on Brian. January is 4 months away. You must have
something in mind between now and then." I thought for a moment and
told her that I was stumped and goalless at this time. That's when she
said those dreaded words, "Why don't you run a 5K?" I told her that I
hated running unless it was chasing a fuzzy tennis ball. Running for the
sake of running was definitely not my forte. "Great. Then what else can
you do?" she asked. She had me and she knew it. With that, she told me
to get in line and sign up for the 5K resolution run, which takes place on
New Year's Day.

I continued to do my weekly walks at rehab and my daily walks around
my neighbourhood with the 5K goal ahead of me. By the beginning of

October, I gradually went from walking to a walk-jog. The first ratio I was put on was called a 5:1, which meant that I would walk for five minutes and then run for one and repeat until the full distance was completed. As October came to a close, I had to finally move my neighbourhood walks indoor. I joined the local civic centre so that I could walk inside the tennis dome where a track circled four tennis courts. This excited me because those four tennis courts were where I had my first heart episode playing tennis and I was working to get back in January. It felt great to be circling my goal every day as I went around the track doing my walk-jog. On a number of occasions, our tennis pro, Mark, was there. He would smile and wave; he knew that I was trying to move from the track to inside the netting and onto the tennis courts. I really appreciated his silent support every time I saw him.

By mid-November, I made my next advancement in my curriculum and was promoted to doing a 3:1 now. Shortly after this, I traveled to San Diego on business for a week and luckily, I was able to take Lori with me. The downside was that my schedule was so busy; I didn't have time to get to the hotel gym. It felt weird not being able to do my daily regime that week. When I returned from my business trip, I got right back into my routine. I couldn't believe that taking one week off from my normal routine was so painful. That first 3:1 felt like I was starting from scratch.

The following week, I went to a client dinner meeting at Ruth Chris Steakhouse and was able to bring Lori, which was awesome since it was a nice restaurant. It was my first time out with my customer in this type of setting since my surgery. When we placed our orders, I asked for a petit filet. The other members at our table began laughing hysterically. You see, not that long ago, I was in a similar setting a few years ago. I was challenged to order the 72oz steak, which of course, I did. They bet that I would never eat it all, which of course, I did. Remember, I'm a little competitive. In fact, I even took one bite out of my challenger's 72oz steak that he couldn't finish - just to prove my point. But alas, those days were way behind me now; I had heart surgery. There were changes that I needed to make and this was just one of them. The rest of the night was great and I was quite full after eating my petit steak.

The following day, I was back at the track and doing my routine when I bumped into a tennis colleague from our league. He asked if I wanted to have a friendly match that is if my recovery was up to it. At my next rehab appointment, I asked Rajeanne and she said, "as long as it's a "friendly" match, it shouldn't be a problem. Just monitor yourself with your heart rate monitor and ensure that your heart rate is recovering well." With that green light, I played my friendly game of tennis on December 14th. It felt great to be back on the court. There were a number of shots that I would normally chase down, but I didn't; I wanted to heed the advice that I had been given. This made me hungrier to get back to my ultimate goal of competitive tennis. At least I played the full hour without any shortness of breath incidents, which felt awesome. It's been a long time since I felt that way.

Just before Christmas, I went to see my family doctor for a routine check-up; he was still monitoring me post-surgery. He was ecstatic with my cholesterol results. My LDL, or lousy cholesterol reading, went down to 1.5 and my HDL, or happy cholesterol reading, was at 2.5. He recommended that I should take up yoga so that I wasn't just focusing on my physical recovery but my mental recovery as well. I accepted his advice and said that I would make it happen. He commented and said that he wished that all of his patients were as motivated as me.

A week and half later, on December 30th, I ran my first 1:1, which was good timing since the resolution 5K run was only two days away. I felt like I had done all that I could do to prepare for this goal, so I took New Year's Eve off to rest up for the big run.

On New Year's Day, Lori drove me to the YMCA in Oshawa to do the 5K. As it turns out, the weather wasn't going to cooperate; we had some snow overnight and the streets were covered with 3 to 4 inches of slush, nice! I went in, registered and got my running bib with number 1350 on it. I couldn't help but think that this was a great way to start of the New Year and finally put 2007 and all of its anguish and anxiety behind me. I also met one of Lori's work colleagues, Steven, who was an avid runner. We chatted for a bit. He said that he couldn't run with me since my pace would be too slow, which I fully understood since he had a pace that he needed to adhere to and this broken guy was nowhere near his calibre. He took me out to the starting line and when the gun went off, he wished me luck and said, "See you at the finish line Brian. You are a true inspiration to us all!"

After a few meters, I was running beside another lady and shared some pleasantries. She asked me why I was running, so I shared my story and journey with her. She said that she was totally touched by my story and then explained that she was a nurse. She also asked that if I didn't mind, she would like to run with me to make sure I am okay. I jumped at that offer; it immediately made me feel that much better about completing this run in one piece. She was great company for me and we chatted most of the way - mostly complaining about the slush and how cold our feet were. Oh well, no pain, no gain I guess.

When we were about a kilometer from the finish line, I saw someone running the wrong way and right towards us. It turned out to be Steven. He asked that if I didn't mind, could he run the last bit with me and cross the finish line with today's hero. I choked back some tears, said sure and introduced him to my running mate. When I came across the finish line, Lori snapped a photo of my running mate and me as I raised my arms in triumph.

After that, I took a couple of days off of my regular rehab routine to recover from achieving another huge recovery goal, recover both physically and emotionally. On January 6th, my daughter Julie said that she would like to come to the track and run with me, which I thought would be great to have some company to run with and it was time to get back on the horse, so to speak. We ran 3 miles that day, which felt great, and Julie did a really good job keeping up with me. Darn 17 year olds. They just seem to be able to pick up and run whenever they want, but as it turns out, she was having a real tough time walking around the next day because she was in some considerable pain. We joked about how this middle aged heart survivor was in better shape than her, which made me realize just how far I have come along with my recovery in the last nine months.

Two days later, on January 8ᵗʰ, I picked up my tennis bag, my shoes and hat and walked out the front door to go back to the scene of the crime. I was going to play competitive tennis for the first time after my surgery. It had been nine and half months since my surgery and I was so excited, but very nervous. Coming back brought back so many memories of what I had endured over the past year and it was hard to believe that this day had finally arrived. I was, of course, at the bottom of the tennis ladder to start, but I didn't care. I was back in the game and that was the goal and I would work on my ladder positioning down the road. For now, I just wanted to make sure that playing at a competitive level was possible.

As I parked at the civic centre and made my long walk to the tennis dome, I became rather emotional and had a few tears running down my cheek. I wiped them away and made the trek into the tennis dome. The trip felt totally different and it had a very special feeling to it. Our tennis pro, Mark, was there, shook my hand, welcomed me back and said that I had been missed.

With that, I was back on the courts and playing a match. As I did with my friendly match, there were some balls that I didn't attempt to get, but overall, I was pleased with my physical performance. What pleased me the most was that the shortness of breath problem was finally gone. I watched my heart rate the entire night as it got high as 132, but it always recovered nicely. I walked off the court that night with tears streaming down my cheeks. But that was okay, nobody could tell as it just mixed in with all the sweat that was running down my face as well.

I did it. I completed my three immediate goals that I set in my cardiac rehab. I did the 60K charity walk four and half months after my surgery, the 5k run nine months after my surgery and now, I played competitive tennis nine and half months after my surgery. I couldn't have been happier. At my last rehab appointment the following week, Rajeanne congratulated me for all that I had accomplished and said that I was one of the most inspirational patients she had ever had. She handed me my graduation diploma and a gold heart pin. She leaned in and whispered, "So what's your next goal?" I told her that I was running a 10K on April 27th, the one year anniversary of my surgery. She just smiled and said, "I never had a doubt. You would take it up another notch."

As I pulled out of the hospital parking lot for the last time that night, I reflected on the last six months and everything that I had accomplished. I truly believe that everyone, who has a heart incident and is offered a chance to take a cardiac rehabilitation program, should run at the chance - no pun intended. I can't imagine where my life would have been if I didn't take this opportunity to heart. Okay, pun was intended here.

As for the 10K run, I couldn't find a run anywhere in the greater Toronto area for April 27th. I was stuck and didn't know what to do. I know that you're probably thinking that I could have just let that defeat this goal for me but then, you have probably came to the conclusion that I'm a bit of a goal guru. So instead, I invented my own 10K run and selfishly called it the "Brian Campkin Invitational 10K Run!" I mapped out a run from my house to my daughter's high school and back again; it just happened to be exactly 10K. On April 27, 2008, one person showed up for this race. And I came in first, second and third. Now that's owning the podium!

Pre-run 5K

Crossing the finish line of the 2008 5K Resolution Run with Jennifer who I met that day

A shot of the track around the tennis courts at the Civic Centre

Back on the courts at the Oshawa Civic Tennis Dome

Back on the courts but surrounding them was the track where I did
all of my indoor recovery walks

With my trophy for winning the Summer 2008 mixed doubles championship, 1 year after my surgery

On court #1 where all my troubles started. Standing with Mark Krycia our tennis pro who was instrumental in getting me back to competitive tennis

Cinnamon Apple Bread Pudding

Ingredients
4 cups (1L) cubed whole grain bread
2 eggs
2 egg whites
3/4 cup (175mL) unsweetened applesauce
1/2 cup (125mL) skim milk
2 tsp (10mL) ground cinnamon
1/2 cup (125 mL) low fat vanilla yogurt
1 small apple, cored and diced
Ground cinnamon (optional)

Directions

Sprinkle bread in sprayed 8 inch(2 L) square baking dish; set aside. In bowl, whisk together eggs, egg whites, applesauce, milk and cinnamon. Pour over bread and press bread gently into egg mixture. Bake in 375°F(190°C) oven for 30 minutes or until golden, puffed and knife inserted in centre comes out clean.

Serve each piece with dollop of yogurt, apple and sprinkling of cinnamon, if using.

Tip: You will need about 4 slices of whole grain bread to get the 4 cups(1 L).

Nutritional Analysis per serving (about 1/2 cup (125 mL) (each)

Calories: 112

Protein: 6 g

Total fat: 3 g

Saturated fat: 1 g

Cholesterol: 48 mg

Carbohydrate: 18 g

Fibre: 2 g

Sugar: 8 g

Sodium: 157 mg

Potassium: 164 mg

Recipe developed by Emily Richards, P.H. Ec. The Heart and Stroke Foundation 2011

Chapter 12 – Making a Difference, Brian the Volunteer

"Never doubt that a small group of thoughtful committed citizens can change the world; indeed, it's the only thing that ever has."

~ Margaret Mead
Cultural Anthropologist, 1901 – 1978.

As I began my cardiac rehabilitation work, I was also engaging with the Heart and Stroke Foundation as a volunteer and survivor speaker. My chance meeting with the Heart and Stroke Foundation at my customers' golf tournament in June, 2007 definitely paid off because I was introduced into the Ontario Chapter Office in downtown Toronto. I was eagerly excited to see how I could take advantage of my second chance and give back.

I began working with the Ontario office in September, 2008. My very first engagement was at the Department of National Defence base in Toronto; they were doing a pancake breakfast fundraiser in support of the Heart and Stroke. This event was sort of like a homecoming for me. I called all of the Department of National Defence bases in Ontario in a previous sales role ten years earlier. The event went well and I received some very nice accolades from the organizer of the base and my representative from the Heart and Stroke office. I never felt such an exhilarating rush as I did when I shared my story. I couldn't help but feel that it was likely due to me dedicating my volunteer efforts to my Dad and Mike.

Later in December, I was introduced to the local Durham Region Heart and Stroke office and met with their area manager and some of her staff. They immediately had two opportunities for me. First, I was asked if they could print my story and place it on the caravan awareness booths that were located in a few shopping malls across the area. Secondly, they wanted me to speak at a volunteer appreciation event at a local theatre. I jumped at both of these opportunities.

Then, they introduced me to the President of their local volunteer council, Brenda Benedet, who asked both Lori and I to join their volunteer leadership council, which we both did. Boy, this was becoming exciting and quite busy at the same time. I was really pouring myself into my volunteerism and thought that volunteering was something you retired into when you have time on your hands, like my Mom after she left the workforce. I realized that you don't have to wait and there's plenty to do; and you are greatly appreciated.

My first big project for the Foundation's Ontario office was working with June Rogers, their National Editor, Web and Publications. She wanted me to write a blog for the Heart and Stroke web site that would be published on a monthly basis over the next year. She wanted me to share my journey with heart disease from my symptoms and diagnosis to recovery road and beyond. This ended up being a wonderful opportunity for me. It became very therapeutic for me to write about my experience and I was really glad that I had kept a journal about my journey during the first year of my recovery. In fact, I would highly recommend it for anyone going through a similar journey; a journal can be very rewarding and good therapy for your recovery. Writing this blog also became the catalyst for my passion to write this book, so I have a lot to thank June for. She also went on to be my "book coach" and strongly encouraged me. She told me that I was gifted and needed to make this book happen. She saw something that I didn't see in myself, which happens quite often in life.

Early 2008, my volunteer efforts really began to take off. We were asked if my family could be placed on a brochure that the HSF were putting together. And on the day I got back to competitive tennis, a photographer came to take some photos of our family, including Jackson, which was awesome. The next day, I was off to the Rogers' head office to tape a P.S.A, or public service announcement, for the foundation. It was a cool opportunity and beforehand, we were given a tour of the CHFI radio station and spoke with the on air disc jockey. He thanked me for my efforts and wished me well. He also shared a story about his Dad and how he was impacted by heart disease, which became a reoccurring theme for me in my volunteer efforts. It seemed that everyone had a common story regarding heart disease, which motivated me even more to make a difference. A few weeks later while driving down the road, I heard my voice on the radio. It was pretty freaky to be behind the wheel of your car minding your own business listening to the radio and then, your voice comes on. It made me feel quite proud.

In early February, I was interviewed by the local community newspaper in support of the Heart and Stroke heart month report. It was published on Sunday, February 3rd, which was also Super Bowl Sunday. It was a full page story - complete with my picture - and focused on how I motivated myself to get back on the tennis court. When I went to a local establishment later that afternoon to watch the Super Bowl, the owner came over because she recognized me from the paper and offered our table a free round of beverages complete with some promotional hats and shirts. Wow, I had no idea that my volunteering would take on this sort of celebrity type status; it really became quite a fun experience.

The following week, I was invited to the local Rogers T.V. studio to be interviewed for heart month. It was about a five minute interview. The host was so impressed with my story that he invited me to come back to do a 15 minute segment a couple of weeks later. When the HSF heard, they were thrilled to get the extra air time and exposure. Man, I was really making a difference now. I started to realize that my story was motivational and was making others take notice of themselves and the changes they needed to make in their lives for the better.

My first heart month was starting to get really busy as I began attending heart month kick offs at the local Boston Pizza restaurants; they were a big supporter and made heart shaped pizzas in support of the HSF. Brenda, the council president, attended one of these events and I was able to meet her husband Leonard. It was there that a long standing friendship started to blossom. Of course, like all other relationships in my life, they really took off once they met Lori, which took place at the local theatre's fundraising event that I spoke at. Like they say, "Behind every successful man is a great woman," which was definitely the case.

I did my second local newspaper interview the following month. The Oshawa community paper also wanted to pick up on the story that was published earlier in Whitby. The events didn't stop as we moved out of heart month. The next series of events was the Jump Rope and Hoops for Heart at the local schools, which quickly became my favourite events. The hardest part was finding a way to relate to this type of an audience. So I decided to leverage my girl's stories from my blog. I always get a bit emotional when I read their stories, but I think it made the message more powerful and relatable. Speaking in front of a school gymnasium full of kids from kindergarten to grade 8 was really rewarding. I felt like I was making a difference at an earlier age and making a bigger impact. I spoke at seven schools in all and some even sent me some wonderful thank you letters. The best part was the question and answer session. Kids had great questions like, "Were you awake for your surgery?" "Can we see your scars?" "Did it hurt?" and others.

At the end of March, I was invited to speak at the Heart and Stroke CEO Appreciation event at the top of the RBC Plaza in downtown Toronto. I was pretty nervous since I shared the stage with the CEO of the HSF at the time, Rocco Rossi, whom I had never met. Rocco was a terrific speaker, which made me even more nervous since I had to follow him. The room was set up as a cocktail reception setting with 200 or so guests standing around a number of cocktail tables. As I finished my speech, there was a thunderous applause. I told everyone that it was my first standing ovation. Rocco shook my hand afterwards and thanked me for such a heartfelt message. I told him that he could count on me to partake in more events for him. On the way home, Lori said that it was my best speech to date.

On the way home, I couldn't stop thinking about how much Rocco's public speaking really impressed me. At our next council meeting, I shared this with Brenda, who was also a professional development coach. She told me that I should join a Toastmasters club if I wanted to get better. I took her advice, like I did so with all my doctors, and did exactly that in order to be a better volunteer survivor speaker.

Locally, I attended the Roger Weir Hockey for Heart event and was a part of the cheque presentation program. I never thought that I would be meeting celebrities in my travels. At this event, I got to meet retired Toronto Maple Leaf players Darryl Sittler and Wendel Clark. Lori was thrilled to meet Jim Cuddy from Blue Rodeo, which just happened to be one of her favourite Canadian bands. Being a volunteer was starting to have some benefits for sure!

My volunteer efforts continued throughout the year as I spoke at volunteer appreciation events, AED plaque presentation events and other local community events. Later that fall, I was invited to speak at the Heart and Stroke Foundation internal program coordinator and area manager's kick-off event for their new fiscal year. I was truly looking forward to this one because I got to share the stage with Rocco again and I wanted to let the staff at the HSF know how important they are to a survivor like me. I received some awesome feedback from the staff after my speech; most of them said that I had reinvigorated them in their jobs. It felt pretty good to give back to the foundation this way. By the end of the summer, my story and pictures with Lori, the girls and Jackson were used in the Toronto Star, a national newspaper, for the HSF Lottery insert. Sharing my story was taking on a bigger stage now and it felt great to know that I was reaching a broader audience. In fact, my cardiologist not only congratulated me on my great check-up but also on my work with the HSF - he saw the Toronto Star piece.

I felt quite honoured to have done so much work in such little time for the Heart and Stroke Foundation by the end of the year. Everyone, who I have engaged with, was so nice and appreciative for all the work that we did as volunteers. I ended the year by taping a video of my story for the door-to-door campaign that ran every February and wondered what was in store for me in 2009 and beyond that.

It turned out that my involvement with the Heart and Stroke Foundation flourished from this point forward. My story continues to be shared at many local events, as well as, major events like Ride for Heart and in national publications like The Globe and Mail, Macleans magazine and the Canadian Business magazine. I was also afforded the opportunity to share my story on national T.V. I realized that by dedicating my time and my story, I was impacting Canadians to understand how they may be able to make a change in their life or lifestyles to further their health and time with their loved ones.

In 2010 and 2012, I was formally recognized for my efforts when I won the Heart and Stroke Volunteer Award of Excellence and the Heart of Gold Award. Both plaques hang proudly on my wall as a constant reminder of my second chance at life and my promise to my Dad and Mike that I would honour them and their lives by making a difference and giving back to my community. I continue to volunteer for the Heart and Stroke today and am proud to be named as the official spokesperson of the foundation. In their words, I am an expert survivor.

2010 Volunteer Excellence Award

Ride for Heart photo with Marco Di Buono now V.P. of Science & Research
with the American Heart Assocation

After my surgery I placed the Canada Food Guide I got from the hospital on my fridge, where it remains to this day

At an AED Induction ceremony where I met fellow survivor
and now good friend Susan Edwards.

Cheque presentation at the Hockey for Heart with Rob Weir, Louise Weir and Judith Hartley

Delivering my speech at the ACC home of my Maple Leafs.
Never thought I would speak in their big house, this was an amazing opportunity for me

Doing the Omni TV commercial for Heart Month at the Toronto Eaton Centre

Family photo at ACC with Eric, Kelly, Lori, Julie, Ryan and Megan

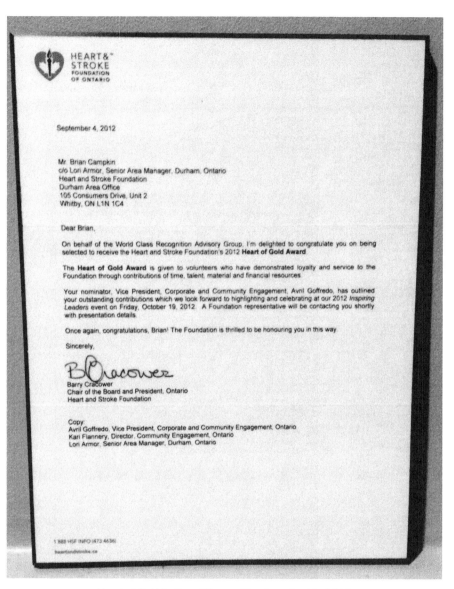

Heart of Gold Letter of Recognition I received in 2012

**HEART &
STROKE
FOUNDATION
OF ONTARIO**

Finding answers. For life.

2300 Yonge Street
Suite 1300
P.O. Box 2414
Toronto, Ontario
M4P 1E4

Tel. (416) 489-7100
Fax (416) 489-6885

HONORARY PATRON
The Honourable
David C. Onley, O.Ont.
Lieutenant Governor
Of Ontario

BOARD OF DIRECTORS
Colleen Johnston, F.C.A.
Chair of the Board and President

Barry Cracower
Vice Chair of the Board

Directors
Chi-Ming Chow, M.D.
U. Phillip Daniels, Ph.D.
Shafiq Ebrahim, M.B.A.
Lisa Heidman, LL.B.
Michael A. Kessel, MBA
Marlys L. Koschinsky, Ph.D.
Michael LeClair
G. Peter Oakes, C.A.
Donna Parr
Richard C. Pettit, C.A.
J. Geoffrey Pickering, M.D.
Margaret L. Rand, Ph.D.
Allan Reynolds

Honorary Director
Anthony Graham, M.D.

CHIEF EXECUTIVE OFFICER
David W. Sculthorpe

FOUNDATION SECRETARY
Pauline Wijeyesekera

August 25th, 2010

Brian Campkin
c/o Bob Leonhardt, Area Manager, Durham
Heart and Stroke Foundation of Ontario
105 Consumers Drive, Unit 2
Whitby, ON L1N 1C4

PRIVATE & CONFIDENTIAL

Dear Brian,

On behalf of the World Class Recognition Advisory Group, I'm delighted to congratulate you on being selected to receive the Heart and Stroke Foundation of Ontario's 2010 **Heart and Stroke Award for Volunteer Excellence**.

The **Heart and Stroke Award for Volunteer Excellence** is given to a volunteer who has proudly advocated the Foundation's mandate and heightened its profile through fundraising, volunteer development or mission activities. Not only are you being recognized for your vision, but for your strategic ability to make each vision a reality. You have added incredible value to the Foundation by demonstrating leadership excellence, delivering on commitments and contributing to high-quality results.

Your nominator, Jennifer Woodill, has outlined your outstanding contributions which we look forward to highlighting and celebrating at HSFO's 2010 Annual General Meeting (AGM) on Friday, November 19th, 2010 (4:00pm - 5:30pm, with reception to follow). A Foundation representative will be contacting you shortly with presentation details.

Once again, congratulations! The Foundation is thrilled to be honouring you in this way.

Sincerely,

Colleen Johnston
Chair of the Board and President
Heart and Stroke Foundation of Ontario

cc: Jennifer Woodill, Bob Leonhardt, Judith Fowler, Avril Goffredo

www.heartandstroke.ca
1-888-HSF-INFO (473-4636)

Business Number 10747 2839 RR0001

HSFO Award for Volunteer Excellence

Joanie, Lori and I at the Put Your Heart Into It kick off at Nathan Phillips Square

June Rogers and I at Ride for Heart

Lori and I at the 2012 Ride for Heart

Lori and I participating in Susan's 2011 Big Bike event

Lori and I riding up the Don Valley Parkway at the 2011 Ride for Heart event

Lori and I with Avril Goffredo of the Heart and Stroke Foundation

Lori and I with Jim Cuddy from Blue Rodeo at the Hockey for Heart event

Lori and I, Team Tin Man at the 2011 Ride for Heart

Lori and Joanie with Joanne Cullen of the HSF during a heart month event
at Nathan Phillips Square in Toronto

Lori and Susan at one of the many heart month rallies we volunteered at

HEART AND STROKE FOUNDATION OF ONTARIO

Award for
Volunteer Excellence

Recognizing Heart and Stroke Foundation of Ontario
volunteers for their vision, strategic ability, leadership
excellence, commitment, high quality results and proud
advocacy of the Foundation's mandate and work to
heighten the Foundation's profile.

Presented to

Brian Campkin

2010

HEART &
STROKE
FOUNDATION
OF ONTARIO
Finding answers. For life.

My 2010 Volunteer Award of Excellence

Whitby man makes up his mind to live well

Proof attitude is everything

stories of
inspiration

Brian Campkin credits a positive attitude for his recovery from heart surgery

Judi Bobbitt
jbobbitt@durhamregion.com

DURHAM -- When Brian Campkin opened the Heart and Stroke Foundation pamphlet, there was the stark truth in black and white: For 50 per cent of people diagnosed with heart disease, the first symptom is death.

Mr. Campkin was among the more fortunate 50 per cent.

Eight years ago, at the age of 46, the Whitby man looked and felt fairly fit. He was not a smoker, wasn't overweight, and his bloodwork checked out fine -- he didn't have high cholesterol, diabetes or any other condition that can plague the middle-aged. He was a self-described "weekend warrior", enjoying tennis regularly.

Then one day, while warming up for a competitive tennis match, Mr. Campkin was unable to breathe. His wife cajoled him into seeing his doctor, and five weeks of tests brought the news that three arteries in his heart were nearly completely blocked. He would need triple bypass surgery.

"The first emotion is fear," recalls Mr. Campkin over coffee, looking back at the journey which has brought him to the role of motivational speaker and soon-to-be author.

Fully expected the doctor to tell him he was just experiencing stress, and to take some time off work. But with his wife dissolving into tears at the diagnosis and the future suddenly very uncertain, Mr. Campkin was shocked and afraid.

The fear is not knowing."

Though the actor John Ritter died of a recent condition -- a tear in his aorta -- in 2003, the comedian was very much on Mr. Campkin's mind as he was going into surgery. Mindful that Mr. Ritter had been "jovial funny" to the end, Mr. Campkin decided to hide behind humour. It was one of several decisions he consciously made, not the least of which was making up his mind to be going to be just fine.

Having lost his own father to a heart attack at a young age, and having attended the funeral of a friend who died of a heart attack at 48, Mr. Campkin gave his own situation serious thought.

"I had to question where I was and where he was," he says of his friend, whose funeral was the most difficult he'd experienced. "I was given a second chance for a reason. I was going to make a difference with that second chance. I've never forgotten."

Even before he woke up from the five-hour heart surgery -- the story goes he woke up asking for a pina colada -- Mr. Campkin was suggesting to the Heart and Stroke Foundation he become one of its speakers. He had read the literature, researched the information available and "I set my sights on recovery road. What's in my control is how to have the proper recovery. That's in my control."

Mr. Campkin set his goals and began to work toward them: He wanted to do a 60k charity walk; he wanted to play competitive tennis again, and he wanted to be around to walk all three of his daughters down the aisle.

He began by walking "one crack in the sidewalk farther" daily, and was able to do the charity walk 4.5 months after surgery. He ran 5k nine months after surgery, and was playing tennis again in under 10 months. In November 2011, he walked his first daughter down the aisle.

He revamped his lifestyle where he could after the surgery, losing 20 pounds, being mindful of eating well, and exercising regularly. He keeps setting new goals and wants to enjoy an active life with his grandchildren. He rides in the annual Heart and Stroke Foundation's Ride for Heart on the Don Valley Parkway in Toronto, being held this year June 1.

In the meantime, he's become an enthusiastic speaker for the Heart and Stroke Foundation and shares his message with audiences whenever he can. He became a member of the Canadian Association of Professional Speakers and it led to the opportunity to write a book with the Heart and Stroke Foundation, which he says will have "two voices": hope and prevention.

"If I can help one family or one person not go through the hardship and pain we went through, I'm overpaid as a volunteer.

"A positive mental attitude is the crux of your success," he says earnestly. "Every day has bad moments, but don't make it a bad day. It's not what happens to you, it's how you react."

Mr. Campkin knows genetics was the wild card in his own brush with death, and he urges everyone to be aware of their risk factors, listen to their own body and take whatever steps can be taken today to ensure a healthier tomorrow and a good quality of life.

"Set a goal, put it in motion, tell everybody about it and watch it evolve," he says. "The more we try to show up as who we are, the better the world is.

"Goals aren't a destination. They're a journey."

Stories of Inspiration will appear monthly in 2014. If you have an inspiring story you'd like us to consider sharing with readers, e-mail Judi Bobbitt at jbobbitt@durhamregion.com.

DURHAM -- Brian Campkin of Whitby credits a positive attitude for his recovery after triple bypass heart surgery and his resulting work with the Heart and Stroke Foundation as a motivational speaker and author.
Submitted photo

My article in the Whitby this Week May 2014

My introduction slide from the 2012 Heart of Gold awards,
I chose the word attitude as my introduction

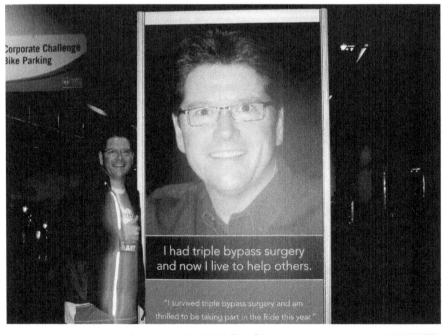

My poster at the 2010 Ride for Heart event

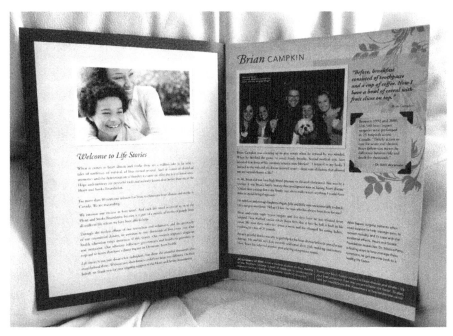

Our family photo and story to support the HSF in the Life Stories pamphlet

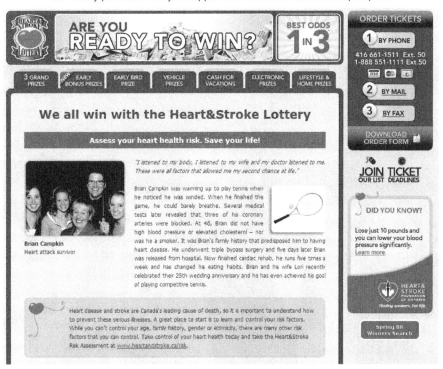

Our family photo in the Toronto Star Heart and Stroke Lottery advertisement

Photo taken after my presentation at a local Boston Pizza restaurant in support of heart month

Photo the HSF had taken of our family for future volunteer opportunities and articles

Picture of my appearance on Breakfast Television in Feburary of 2014

My induction into Toastmasters wtih VP of Education Irene Konzelmann

Picture from the 2011 Ride for Heart campaign

Picture of my poster at the 2012 Ride for Heart wrap up venue

Presenting an award to the top volunteers for the
Canadian Tire Jump Start program in Ajax, Ontario

Presnenting at one of the many Heart Month kick off events in Durham Region

Receiving my gift after speaking at the Sault Ste. Marie volunteer appreciation event

Receiving the Bowmanville Toastmaster Speaker of the Year award in 2011 from Dave Deveau

Skating with Eric, Kelly, Lori, Megan, Ryan and Carelton the Bear at the ACC

Speaking at one of the many local Heart and Stroke events in Durham Region

Speaking at the Portraits of Giving event in 2011

Speaking at the Soiree for Heart event

Susan and I at her 2013 Big Bike ride, love the survivor paddles!

Susan and I with one of my favourite Toronto Maple Leaf players,
Wendell Clark at the Hockey for Heart event

Team photo of the 7 Summit climbers that was in the Toronto Globe and Mail newspaper

HEART &
STROKE
FOUNDATION
Finding answers. For life.

October, 2010

Brian Campkin
133 Ardwick Street
Whitby, ON L1N 9H5

Dear Brian,

I would like to extend our sincere and heartfelt appreciation for your commitment to the mission of the Heart and Stroke Foundation of Ontario. In particular, thank you for speaking to our Program Coordinators, Area Managers and partners in the provinces across Canada at our Fiscal 2011 training meetings.

The stories and experiences that you shared during your keynote address were simply inspiring. Your moving account of how you were empowered after your surgery to communicate the importance of living a healthy lifestyle, to raise funds in support of the mission and to demonstrate to your family, friends and colleagues how they too can help make a difference in their lives and communities, was powerful . Your words will be instrumental in helping our staff to build on the experiences that they have to empower volunteers in their communities.

Once again, I thank you for your ongoing support and participation with our organization and I wish you and your family continued heart health!

Sincerely,

David Sculthorpe
Chief Executive Officer

2300 Yonge Street
Suite 1300
Toronto, Ontario M4P 1E4
Tel. (416) 489-7100
Fax (416) 489-6885
e-mail: mail@hsf.on.ca

www.heartandstroke.ca
1-888-HSF-INFO (473-4636)

Thank you Letter from David Sculthorpe CEO of the Heart and Stroke
for one of the speeches I delivered

Reic'd May 1/08

Durham District School Board
Uxbridge Public School
64 Victoria Drive
Uxbridge, Ontario

L9P 1H2

905-852-9101

Principal: *A. Young, B.A., B.Ed. ,M.Ed.*   Vice-Principal: *V. Brooks, B.Ed., BPHE*

Tuesday April 29th 2008

Dear Brian,

I would like to take this opportunity to thank you for coming to our school today to share your story about heart disease. The grade 6, 7, and 8 students had the chance to see how vital it is to raise money for the Heart and Stroke Foundation. When the students can put a real face and name to the disease, they can see how it can affect that individual and their family. The stories you shared from your 3 daughters were extremely powerful as the students could relate and reflect on how they would feel if they were in that situation. The students listened intently as you shared your goals, fears, and successes before and after your surgery. I know they also very much appreciated the time you took to answer their questions and share your knowledge about living a healthy lifestyle and listening to one's body. I know that this very personal story will encourage our students to put forth an extra effort when they fundraise for the Heart and Stroke Foundation this year because of your story.

Thank you once again from the staff and students of Uxbridge Public School,

Christina Gibb (teacher co-ordinator)

Thank you letter from Uxbridge Public School after speaking at their
Jump Rope for Heart Event in 2008

The Globe and Mail article from Feb 2014 where my story was utilized
for the most recent study from the HSF

Volunteering and sharing my story at one of the Caravan events during heart month in 2008

Volunteering during Heart Month

With Barry Cracower, Chair of the Board of HSF and Tom McAllister, COO of HSF at Heart of Gold award ceremony

With David Sculthorpe CEO of the Heart and Stroke Foundation with Nacho Figueros, Lori and I at the Polo for Heart event

With David Sculthorpe, CEO of the Heart and Stroke Foundation at the Heart of Gold Awards

With fellow survivor Sheryl Gill who I teamed up with on my first Ride for Heart event

With fellow volunteer, survivor and good friend Shishir at the Heart of Gold ceremony

With Julie, Lori, Megan and Ryan at the Soiree for Heart event

With my Heart and Stroke Volunteer Award of Excellence I recevied in November of 2010

With my very good friend and fellow volunteer Brenda Benedet

With Brenda and Leonard Florida January 2014

With Olympian Curt Harnett and former CEO of the HSF, Rocco Rossi at the Ride for Heart event

With Ryan, Megan, Julie and Lori at the Soiree for Heart event I spoke at

With Susan Edwards and Judith Hartley at Durham Heart Month event

With the Durham Region HSF staff and volunteers at the
Oshawa Heart Month Rally that I spoke at

Raspberry Banana Sorbet Cups

Ingredients
1 large very ripe banana, chopped
2 tbsp (25 mL) icing sugar
2 cups (500 mL) frozen raspberries
1/4 tsp (1 mL) ground cinnamon
3 sheets phyllo pastry
Fresh mint leaves

Directions

Lay one sheet of phyllo on work surface and spray lightly with cooking spray. Sprinkle with half of the cinnamon. Lay second sheet on top and repeat spray, sprinkle remaining cinnamon. Top with remaining phyllo and spray with cooking spray. Using a sharp knife cut phyllo into 12 equal pieces. Top 1 square with another, turning a quarter turn to create a flower shape and press into a muffin tin. Repeat with remaining squares to create 6 phyllo cups. Bake in preheated 400° F (200°C) oven for 3 to 4 minutes or until golden. Let cool completely.

Place banana and icing sugar into food processor and puree until smooth. Add raspberries and puree until smooth, soft sorbet forms. Spoon sorbet into cups and garnish with mint if desired.

Nutritional Analysis per serving (1 cup/250 mL)
Calories 80
Protein 1 g
Total Fat 1 g
Saturated Fat 0 g
Cholesterol 0 mg
Carbohydrates 18 g
Fibre 3 g
Sugars 7 g
Sodium 47 mg
Potassium 151 mg

Recipe developed by Emily Richards,
P.H. Ec. © Heart and Stroke Foundation 2013.

Chapter 13 – Milestones and Setbacks

"They say that life is a highway and its milestones are the years, and now and then there's a toll-gate where you buy your way with tears."

~ Joyce Kilmer
American Writer, 1886 – 1918.

When we lose a loved one, we have a difficult time enduring the year of the firsts - that first year without that particular person at Christmas, birthdays, anniversaries and other major milestone events that year. For me, however, there were other firsts that I had set for myself outside of these magical and mystifying dates.

One was to get back on the golf course, my second passion next to tennis. My cardiologist stated that it usually took a minimum of six weeks to recovery from heart surgery before you can test your healing and swing a club.

Five weeks after my surgery, which fell on Father's Day weekend, just so happened to be the same weekend of an annual golf pilgrimage that my brother-in-law, Rob, and I went on every year with 14 other guys.

I decided that I would go again this year, but promised Lori that I was only going as a spectator and would not be playing since I haven't healed sufficiently yet. She made Rob promise her that I would be true to my word and with that, we headed 45 minutes north to our favourite golf and country club.

Friday afternoon, the guys went out for their first round of 18 holes. The golf course graciously provided me my own golf cart, free of charge, so that I could ride around and visit the boys and be a part of the weekend. The 17th hole was our favourite because this course had a replica of all the top signature professional golf holes from around the world. It was the island green from TPC Saw Grass in Florida, which was about a 110 yard hole that you hit to a green, which was surrounded by water.

When I pulled up, all of the foursomes were there to cheer our previous group onto the green. I got out of the cart and walked to the back of Rob's cart and I grabbed a tee, golf ball and his driver. As I walked up to the tee box, he looked over and said, "Hey Bri! What are you doing with my club?" I said that it was time to give this game a test and teed up my ball. He came rushing over to stop me and reminded me about my promise to Lori. I replied, "I told her that I wouldn't be playing a round of golf. I never said that I wouldn't play one hole now did I?" He backed off and asked why I was using a driver to hit a ball just over a hundred yards. I told him that I wasn't sure how much strength I had so I needed the club to do most of the work.

The other fourteen guys were watching and I could tell by the look on their faces that they were settling in for a good laugh, which motivated me even more to tackle this hole. I put my ball on the tee, licked my index finger of my right hand and held it up to see if the wind was my ally. I backed away from the ball and told my group that my first swing wasn't going to count; I needed to use it as a gauge to see how much pain I was going to endure and see if I could hit the ball that far. They afforded me the mulligan as I approached the ball and took a few light practice swings.

I hoped that they couldn't see me wincing behind my sunglasses every time I swung the club because it hurt like hell. But there was no turning back. I stepped over the ball, gripped the club and took a mighty swing. As soon as I had followed through, I immediately went down on one knee and let out a grunt that sounded like a female tennis player hitting a winning forehand. I slowly lifted my head, removed my sunglasses, wiped a tear out of the corner of my eye and asked my group where the ball went. Then, I noticed that they were all bent over laughing and pointing to a ring of tiny waves where my ball had landed in the water.

Rob said, "Nice try Brian, but let's keep moving. We have one more hole to finish before dinner." I ignored him, went back to his bag, grabbed a ball and proceeded to tee it up. He asked me if I was crazy because I obviously wasn't healed enough to hit a ball yet. I reminded everyone that the last swing was just for practice and to stand back and watch. I knew how much pain that I had to endure to make an effective swing. I was going to take one more crack at this green. Everyone leaned their chins on their folded hands atop of their golf clubs and settled in to watch me one more time.

Once again, I took a couple of practice swings with Rob's oversized number 1 driver and then, swung with all my might. Before I went down on one knee, I let out a mighty gasp. But I kept my head up and watched as my ball went on a giant arc towards the green. As I pulled off my sunglasses to get a better look, I saw my ball land squarely on the green about 40 feet from the cup. I looked at the guys and they all pulled their hands off of their clubs and began giving me a round of what I like to call, "fairway applause," as they do in golf.

I did it; I had gotten my swing back and was ready to continue my journey to playing a full 18 holes. How did I finish that hole? I two putted and shot par for that hole for the first time in my life and to this date and for the last time as well. As the summer progressed, I got back to playing golf. My first stab at playing 18 holes was with my brother-in-law, Mike and my niece, Katie, about a month after my first swing attempt. I asked if we could walk the course instead of taking a cart and they concurred. I thought that it would make my first attempt at playing a full 18 that much more significant if I walked the course. It turned out it to be too much of a lofty goal; I had to pack it on the 11th hole. I was too fatigued to continue.

I finally played a full course the following month and went to Myrtle Beach that next spring with Mike and his neighbour, Terry. I ended up playing nine rounds of golf in six days. It took longer than six weeks to really get back to golf and a few setbacks, but you cannot let those speed bumps deter you from achieving your goals.

Another passion of mine is that I really enjoy water skiing. Now, I'm no expert at this; it's just something that I enjoy doing. When I was still at my rehab I mentioned this to Rajeanne, who checked with the cardiologist on staff and wrote me a long letter stating why I couldn't water ski after heart surgery. It had to do with the water temperatures being cold, your core being bent and the strain on your body amongst other things.

I took that letter to my cardiologist and he agreed with everything, but prefaced it with the fact that it would be appropriate for someone, who was older with heart disease. I asked him if he was giving the green light to give this a try and he said yes. It was awesome because I had one more milestone to go after.

I shared this story a few weeks later with some friends of ours during a dinner party at our house. When I finished, my buddy Scott said, "Camper, if you're going to water ski, then you are doing it behind my boat next summer at my cottage!" I immediately accepted his offer and set my sights on taking my recovery up another notch to meet this goal. Early that summer, Lori and I were fortunate enough to be invited to our other friend's cottage. Once again, I shared my story with them our first night there. Jen's brother, Mike, invited me to try tubing the next day as a precursor to my water skiing opportunity at Scott's cottage, which was only a few weeks away.

The next day, it was sunny and gorgeous outside and shortly after breakfast, we headed down to the dock for the day. Just before lunch Mike got the boat geared up for tubing. I put on a life jacket and jumped in the water. I got myself loaded into the tube and in a moment's notice; Mike was pushing down the throttle and taking me around the bay. He was good about it and went at a less than normal speed since it was just a test and he didn't want me to overdo it.

When I came back onto the dock, I was absolutely worn out. The quick lap around the bay proved to be a bit too much for me at this juncture. I went onto the pontoon boat, lied on a bench and fell asleep for about an hour. I was fine afterwards, but it left me thinking that this was exactly what that cardiologist's letter was referring too. I shook the thought out of my head and set my sites on taking my recovery to the next level so that I could ski at Scott's cottage.

When the weekend at Scott's cottage was upon us, he reminded me that he still wanted to take me skiing to which I replied, "Let's get 'er done!" He went out to prep the boat and got the gear out as I got my bathing suit on. I went out and buckled my life jacket on as I squinted up at the sunny sky and wondered if I was going to be able to meet this goal.

I went behind the boat and waited for him to get the ski rope taunt between the tips of my skis. Lori spotted for me and gave me a thumbs up to which I reciprocated and yelled, "Hit it!" And in an instance, I was coming out of my crouch and bending my knees for impact on the water and shaking the water out of my eyes. I did it; I was standing tall and skiing behind Scott's boat. Once again, I took my positive attitude and great advice from my cardiologist and crushed another milestone. To this date, I have water skied at least once a year and was able to finally get up behind Mike and Jen's boat too.

One thing that I didn't have on my list of goals to accomplish was playing ultimate Frisbee. In fact, I really didn't know what it even was until my daughter, Megan, asked me to join her team with a bunch of her friends from high school. I learned that it's a sport played with a disc and points are scored by passing the disc to a teammate in the opposing team's end zone. It's played on a soccer field and you cover the full length of the field but only half the width.

It didn't sound too hard, so I thought, "What the heck. This could be another good recovery milestone for me." With that in mind, I signed up to join their team. After a first few practices, chasing a disc around the school yard was harder than it looked. I wasn't going to be able to cover the whole field and I wasn't good enough to be one of the handler's, or quarterback, as I referred it to. I decided to be what they called a mid, which meant that I only went out a short distance from the handler in order to receive a pass and keep the disc moving down the field. The cups were the ones, who ran a longer distance in order to catch the disc and move our team further down the field.

When our first game was upon us, it was apparent that our cups were matched up with their better players and as a mid, I was matched up against a 5-foot female, who probably didn't even weigh 100 pounds. I smiled and thought to myself, "This should be easy." On our first possession, I caught a few passes and eventually, one of our cups scored a point for us. We were up 1:0 in the first few minutes of the match. Now it was my turn to be on defence and defend against my female counterpart, but this little thing could move. She was as fast and agile as a water bug. She slipped behind my coverage and caught the disc and scored their first point.

I felt bad as I came off, but they all slapped me on the back and gave me some words of encouragement. I couldn't help but feel like I was in over my head with this 5 foot juggernaut. As the match progressed, she went on to score 5 straight points against me. On my sixth shift, I decided that enough was enough; I was going to cover her like a blanket. As I trotted out onto the field, a light rain began, but we played on. Their team had done a great job moving the disc down the field, but I was able to keep this young lady out of the play. They were about 10 feet from our goal line and I was running to cover her. When I saw her eye the disc, which was in route, I stretched my right leg out and waited for the disc to hit my hand as I placed it in front of her two outstretched hands. That's when I heard it. A god awful "snap" at my left ankle. I went down like I had been shot as I watched the disc go into her hands as she scored her 6th point on me.

I grabbed my ankle and rolled over on my back clutching it as I withered in pain. My teammates helped me off the field and immediately placed an ice pack on my ankle. The young lady came over to see if I was ok, which was nice of her, but I just clenched my teeth and said, "Yeah." I was ticked, but it wasn't her fault that I wasn't quite ready for this type of activity. I would have to chalk this one up as another of my recovery setbacks. After visiting the doctor and getting the diagnosis, I had a high ankle sprain and would be in a walking cast for six weeks and then, off to physiotherapy for a few weeks. I retired from my brief and short ultimate Frisbee career. I did get the sympathy vote as Player of the Game for our team, which really just added insult to injury.

One other physical milestone that I took on during my recovery was in February, 2009 when Rocco Rossi, the CEO of HSF, invited me to join an elite group of corporations to do the 7 Summits climb. It was a fund raising event to climb the seventh tallest financial buildings in downtown Toronto. It would consist of walking up 382 floors, or 7,700 steps. To train for this, I continued my normal walking curriculum, but I also started taking the stairs to my office at work, which was on the fifth floor..

I was also invited to speak at the opening ceremonies, where I would share the stage with super model, Monika Schnarre, and ex-hockey player, Jiri Fischer, who had to retire after suffering a heart incident on the bench of an NHL game. In my speech, I told the audience about my cardiologist's advice about having a healthy relationship with my wife and how I only had to master two flights of stairs. I joked with them that I had no idea what this accomplishment could mean for me today. This brought out a large round of laughter and applause. And after doing some choreographed calisthenics and stretching, we headed off.

The first building on my list was the Commerce Court building, which consisted of 55 flights of stairs. On my way to the stairwell, I ran into three ladies, who talked and thanked me for an awesome, inspiring speech. They asked if they could walk me since I was alone and thought that I could use the company and it would also be safer for me. I accepted their invitation and made our way up.

Climbing the stairs was much more different than walking around my neighbourhood or running on the tennis court, but we all settled in and found a good pace that we could keep up to. We conquered that building and after a couple of hours, we were at our fifth of seven buildings, the TD Canada Trust Tower, which had 52 floors. We met Rocco at the bottom of this building and joined us on the climb. He mentioned that the restaurant, where the wrap up event was being held, was at the top of this building. I joked with him that I was taking the elevator when we came back for that portion of the event.

When we got to the 50th floor, a sudden cramp took over my entire left leg and I could barely walk. Rocco and Eileen Greene supported me on the final two flights and unfortunately, I had to quit the climb - two buildings short of achieving the seven summits. I was disappointed because I wasn't used to failure during my recovery besides the two days I missed in my walking curriculum.

In reflection, I realized that when I woke up that morning, I didn't have to climb any steps and now, I actually climbed 302 floors and 6,067 steps in 2 hours and 36 minutes. I raised some significant funds for a great charity like the Heart and Stroke Foundation. It's important that we continue to set these goals and milestones for ourselves. As I said, "Set a goal, put it into motion, tell everybody about it and watch it evolve. The more we show up as who we are the better the world is."

17th hole at Wooden Sticks where I took my first post surgery golf swing

17th hole at Wooden Sticks where I hit my first golf shot post surgery

Brian Tubing 2008 Post Surgery

Tubing with Kelly and Eric at Coughlin Cottage Summer 2013

Getting ready for my first post surgery water ski at Scott Fraser's cottage in Bancroft, Ontario

Ready to yell hit it, as I do my first water ski at Scott's cottage

Getting up on the first try on my first post surgery water ski!
And they said it could not be done

227

All smiles and thumbs right after getting back to the shore after my first ski!

Skiing at Coughlin cottage in the summer of 2013!

Delivering my keynote at the 7 summits kick off

Doing the 7 Summits warm up with Monika Schnarre and the other participants

Former Detroit Red Wing and fellow survivor Jiri Fischer and I
before the climbing the 7 summits

Photo at the 7 Summits before I attempted to conquer all 7 buildings

With then CEO of the HSF Rocco Rossi before our climb

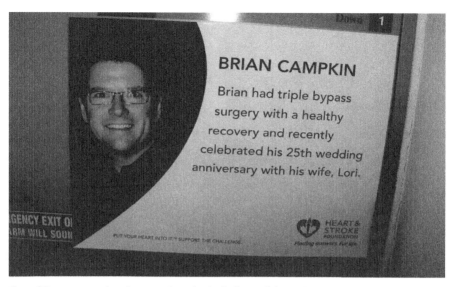

One of the many posters from survivors in the hallway of the staircases at the 7 summits event

With my climbing team at the 7 summits, can't help but notice how wiped I look
and how fresh the ladies look!

With my climbing friends on the floor I had to call it quits.
That's Eileen Greene on my right and Rocco Rossi on my left

Posing in my Christmas gift from my girls in 2013. I love my zipper shirt

Chunky Roasted Vegetable Soup

Ingredients

1 bunch of yellow, orange or
red beets, with greens
Half a head of cauliflower,
chopped
1 carrot, chopped
2 stalks of celery with
leaves, chopped
6 cloves of garlic, minced
1/4 cup (50 mL) orange
juice
2 tsp (10 mL) curry powder
1/2 tsp (2 mL) each ground cumin and coriander
2 tsp (10 mL) canola oil
1 onion, chopped
2 cups (500 mL) sodium reduced vegetable broth
2 cups (500 mL) water

Directions

Cut beet greens off beets, wash well. Chop enough greens to
make 4 cups (1 L) and set aside. Peel beets and chop. Combine
chopped beets, cauliflower, carrot, celery and garlic in a bowl.
Toss with orange juice, curry powder, cumin and coriander to
coat. Spread vegetables onto a parchment paper lined baking
sheet. Roast in a preheated 400 F (200 C) oven for about 30
minutes or until golden and tender crisp.

In a saucepan, heat oil over medium heat and cook onion for about 3 minutes or until softened. Stir in beet greens and cook for about 6 minutes or until wilted. Add roasted vegetables, broth and water. Bring to a boil. Simmer, covered for about 15 minutes or until vegetables are tender.

Nutritional Analysis per serving (1 cup)
Calories 68
Protein 3 g
Total Fat 2 g
Saturated Fat 0 g
Cholesterol 0 mg
Carbohydrates 12 g
Fibre 3 g
Sodium 220 mg
Potassium 414 mg

Recipe developed by Emily Richards,
P.H. Ec. °Heart and Stroke Foundation 2014

Chapter 14 – The Year of the Firsts and No Looking Back

"Patience, persistence and perspiration make an unbeatable combination for success."

- Napoleon Hill
American Author, 1883 – 1970.

set many goals for myself to fully recover. I believe that by setting these goals and achieving them, I was able to achieve many more milestones. Reflecting back, I realize how fortunate I am to have a second chance with my family.

The first milestone was coming from my surgery and having my three daughters stand at the foot of my hospital bed smiling broadly and proudly for what their father had just come through. To say that they were my motivating factor with everything that I have achieved during my recovery would be a huge understatement. Along with my wife, they were the only ones that kept me positive, motivated and inspired to get myself back to being healthier than I was before my surgery. My life goal is to walk each one of my daughters down the aisle on their wedding days.

Two key events took place in the month of June after my surgery. On the 1st, we celebrated Lori's birthday with our three girls by having a nice family dinner at home. That Friday night, we sat around our kitchen table and enjoyed cooking on the rock, which is basically like having a fondue, but in this case, you have a slab of marble that you heat up in the oven and then, you cook your own meal on top of it. We enjoyed snow peas, chicken, steak, potatoes and scallops. I couldn't help but sit back and bask in the moment. I felt so fortunate to be well and to be enjoying some awesome family time. Seventeen days later, Lori and I celebrated our 24th wedding anniversary by going to a local restaurant with my sister, Debbie, and my brother-in-law, Mike, as they had just celebrated their 30th wedding anniversary. It was another significant family moment that I felt blessed to be celebrating.

The following year, Lori and I celebrated our 25th wedding anniversary in fine form by taking a two week vacation to St. Lucia. We shared this milestone with Lori's two brothers, John and Joe, along with their wives Kerry and Sharon. Joe and Sharon had reached their 25th in 2007, while John and Kerry were celebrating theirs, the year after us in 2009. It was great that the six of us spent fourteen gorgeous days in the sunny tropics. Once again, I was thrilled to be checking another key milestone off of my list.

At the end of June, a mere 2 months after my surgery, I was able to achieve another milestone when I went to Kelly's 8th grade graduation and got to do the father – daughter dance with her. I didn't care that the gym lights were bright and that everyone could see my face. I couldn't help but let a tear run down my one cheek as we circled around the dance floor – it was how I felt and I wasn't going to hide it. As they say, real men do cry! I couldn't tell you what song we danced to; in my memory, we were making our own music that night.

As the years rolled on, I had other great moments with Kelly. I watched her flourish in high school in her musical theater class. I had no idea about her passion and talent. She even went on to be in every school play during her tenure in high school. My all-time favourite was her 11th

grade play called, Rocking it Broadway. It happened to be on the night of my birthday and she gave me the best present ever when she sang the finale. She sang *"We Are the Champions"* by Queen, one of my favourite bands from the 70's. She did a great job keeping this from me; it was a total surprise. I was glad that the high school gym was dark as tears flowed down both my cheeks.

Because of my ability to overcome my surgery and deal with heart disease, I was able to see Kelly grow from a young girl into a beautiful woman. She too has had many milestones in her young life that I have been able to witness as well, like getting her driver's licence, graduating from high school and now college, where she will be pursuing a career in early childhood education. I couldn't be more proud of her accomplishments.

I was also able to see my middle daughter, Julie, achieve many things in her life as well. She was in 11th grade, the year that I had my surgery. I got to see her finish with honours for the 3rd year in a row. The following year, she made it a perfect four for four when she graduated with honours. I also got to watch her fly out of our coop when she went off to University to chase her dream. Since then, Julie has moved back home and is about to embark on her last lap of post-secondary school where she will begin a three year program at The Michener Institute of Applied Health Sciences where she will be entering a program in nuclear medicine and molecular imaging. I am really proud of Julie; this program only takes twenty-four students a year and her application was one of them. I look forward to watching her flourish in the program and finally move on into a field that she enjoys.

Megan, my eldest, started university the year of my surgery as she chased her dream of becoming a teacher. It was something she had always aspired to be from the time she was a young child. In fact, when she was growing up and playing school with her cousins, she always insisted on being the teacher. I was extremely proud in the spring of 2010 when Megan graduated from Ryerson University and made Dean's list, which was also amazing to see.

Later that year Megan's high school friend, Ryan, took Lori and I out for a meal. During dessert, he asked if he could have my daughter's hand in marriage. I was fighting back tears when I shook his hand and told him that I couldn't ask for a better son-in-law or husband for my daughter. A little over a year later I hit the jackpot of milestones when I walked Megan down the aisle on November the 12th, 2011. It seemed so surreal for me to have finally hit the biggest goal I had set for myself the moment the doctor told me that I was going to need a triple by-pass. I don't think I have ever smiled that broadly before in my life, that is, when Lori and I became grandparents to our first grandchild, Landon Elliott Boyd, on February 14, 2014.

Looking back now, it has been one helluva journey for me and I couldn't have done it without the support of my caregiving team of doctors, nurses, rehab therapist and my loving family. I am now on a new journey being a grandfather and it is my hope and desire to continue to do what's right for me so that I can enjoy watching Landon and all of my future grandchildren grow up. It isn't my intention to sit on the couch and watch them grow; I want to continue to be fit so that I can get down on the floor and play with him and maybe, take him out on the tennis court and teach him how to play one day.

I truly enjoyed setting and achieving all of the goals I did that first year after my surgery. I think it was paramount to have such a positive experience with heart disease . As I have stated, goals aren't destinations; it's merely a journey onto the next great thing. I still have two daughters to look forward to walking down the aisle on their wedding days and many, many more magical life moments ahead of me.

I believe that when we're at our weakest, we're really achieving our greatest strength and actually the most human. The only thing between you and your goal is you! As George Bernard Shaw said, "The people who get on in this world are the people who get up and look for the circumstances they want, and if they can't find them, they make them!"

Lori's birthday June the 1st and a month after I got home from the hospital

24th Wedding Anniversary 2 months post surgery

Lori and I on our 25th wedding anniversary trip in St. Lucia with her brother Joe and his wife Sharon and her other brother John and his wife Kerry

On our anniversary sunset cruise with Joe, Sharon, John, Kerry, Lori and I

Sharing a laugh with our sunset cruise director!

One of our first sunset anniversary photo's

St. Lucia anniversary sunset photo

We tried to take a sunset photo every night this is just another of those

Lori and I on our anniversary trip to St. Lucia in 2008

Kelly's Grade 8 grad dance June 2007 (2mths post surgery)

Kelly singing her solo - Queen We Are The Champions

Kelly's high school graduation photo

Julie and I before she headed off to her high school prom

Julie and Ryan at their high school graduation in 2008.

Julie and Ryan's send off to University

Lori and I with Megan as she graduated from Ryerson University

Megan and Ryan shortly after their engagement

Dressed as the Tin Man for Megan and Ryan's Jack and Jill costume shower

Finally hitting one of my major life milestones in
walking Megan down the aisle on Nov 12th, 2011

Proud Grandparents showing off the Coffee Mugs they got for Christmas!

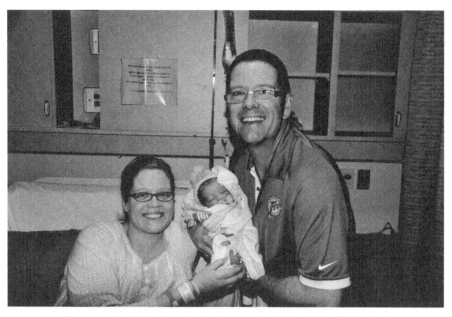

Megan and I with Landon the day he was born in the Belleville Hospital

Gramper Camper with Landon the day he was born, Feb 14, 2014.

Lori and Landon Elliott Boyd Feb. 14, 2014

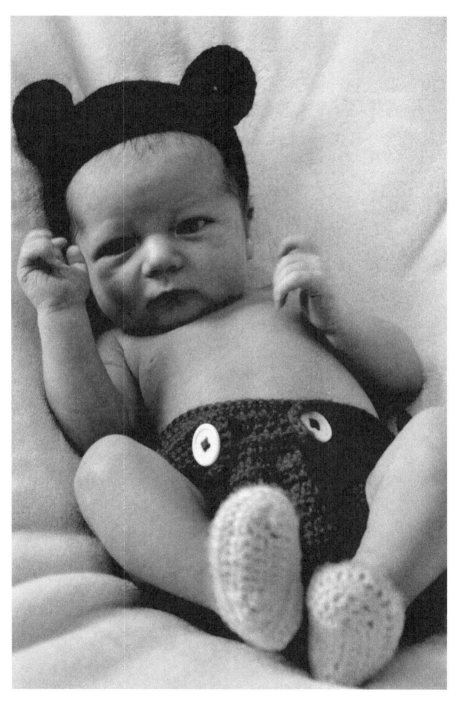

Landon all dressed up as Mickey Mouse

Aunt Julie, Megan, Aunt Kelly with Landon

Landon and I a few weeks after his birth

Grand Mamma with Megan and Landon

Eric, Ryan and I with Landon... called this photo the Boys!

Landon's new born military photo, with Ryan's boots, helmet and dog tags

Landon my little
Maple Leaf!

Landon with the Grampkin's as I have come to call Lori and I

Landon Hot Tub with the Grampkin's

Landon enjoying some Jackson time

The End

Spaghetti and Tuna Pepper Toss

Ingredients
1 pkg (375 g) whole wheat or white fibre spaghetti
2 tsp (10 mL) extra virgin olive oil
1 shallot, chopped
4 cloves garlic, minced
1 each red and yellow or orange pepper, thinly sliced
2 cans (170 g each) canned light tuna in water, drained
1 cup (250 mL) sodium reduced chicken broth
3/4 cup (175 mL) petite cut stewed tomatoes, drained
2 tsp (10 mL) chopped fresh thyme or 1 tsp (5 mL) dried thyme leaves
3 tbsp (45 mL) chopped fresh parsley

Directions
In a large pot of boiling water, cook spaghetti for about 9 minutes or until tender but firm. Drain and return to pot. Meanwhile, in a large nonstick skillet, heat oil over medium heat and cook onions, garlic and peppers for about 4 minutes or until softened. Stir in tuna, broth, tomatoes and thyme and bring to a boil. Simmer for 5 minutes and add to pasta to toss. Stir in parsley and toss again to coat.

Nutritional Analysis per serving (1 1/3 cups or 315 mL)
Calories 306
Protein 10 g
Total Fat 2 g
Saturated Fat 0 g
Cholesterol 12 mg
Carbohydrates 46 g
Fibre 6 g
Sodium 99 mg
Potassium 95 mg

Heart and Stroke Foundation key web links and information

www.heartandstroke.ca

http://www.heartandstroke.ca/Donate

http://www.heartandstroke.ca/Volunteer

http://www.heartandstroke.com/site/c.ikIQLcM-WJtE/b.3484021/k.7C85/Heart_Disease.htm

http://www.heartandstroke.ca/Stroke

http://www.heartandstroke.com/site/c.ikIQLcM-WJtE/b.5374487/k.91C2/Health_eTools.htm

http://www.heartandstroke.ca/Recipes

http://www.heartandstroke.ca/Research

http://www.hc-sc.gc.ca/fn-an/food-guide-aliment/index-eng.php

www.heartandstroke.ca/cpr

Key links to Brian Campkin and to his Volunteer Efforts

http://www.briancampkin.com/

Weekend to End Breast Cancer – Closing Ceremony Keynote:
https://www.youtube.com/watch?v=jTIhh0URiXo

Brian Campkin Make Health Last Interview:
http://www.youtube.com/watch?v=4tsZC68NvuU

Canada Health Infoway: Brian's story:
http://www.youtube.com/watch?v=9aRXZbESbCA

Brian Campkin Heart of Gold Award 2012:
http://www.youtube.com/watch?v=MoReW8M89iI

Make Health Last Brian's Story:
https://www.youtube.com/watch?v=AsT_-vugJiQ

Because of you Brian beat the odds:
https://www.youtube.com/watch?v=aRNuZzJbkX4

Brian Campkin's Journey:

https://www.youtube.com/watch?v=g3EeKo5g-7E

Brian Campkin CTV News Heart Month Interview:

https://www.youtube.com/watch?v=hSQjI0KuZFA

Brian Campkin Air Canada Centre Family Skate – Ride for Heart:

https://www.youtube.com/watch?v=YFc5iI4gGrU

Brian Campkin on Toronto Cares:

https://www.youtube.com/watch?v=Q5NOYQjjr-s

Brian Campkin visits Rogers Daytime – Durham Region:

https://www.youtube.com/watch?v=84kkA0qEm8Q

Brian Campkin - Featured on Family Health - Global TV News:

https://www.youtube.com/watch?v=waS7pVo9xHA

Brian Campkin Heart Month Story – I Will Walk My Daughters Down the Aisle:

https://www.youtube.com/watch?v=qlvV_hIjin0

About the Author

At 46, Brian Campkin was diagnosed with heart disease and required an emergency triple by-pass surgery. From the minute he began his recovery, he knew he wanted to make a difference. As a survivor, he volunteered for the Heart and Stroke Foundation of Canada, speaking to audiences about his struggle to regain his health. Brian has been featured in the Toronto Star, The Globe and Mail, Maclean's magazine and on television and radio. In 2010, the Heart and Stroke Foundation recognized his volunteer excellence and two years later, he received the Heart of Gold award. Brian is married, has three daughters and a grandson.

CPSIA information can be obtained at www.ICGtesting.com
Printed in the USA
LVOW05s2102051214

417467LV00019B/123/P